MW00615581

Salt Water

Salt Water

A Memoir of Remembrance

Lyndsay Wrensen Ph.D., ABD

SALT WATER. Copyright © 2020 by Lyndsay Wrensen. All rights reserved. No part of this book may be reproduced or transmitted in any form or by any means, electronic or mechanical, including photocopying, recording, or by any information storage and retrieval system, without permission in writing from the publisher. Permission to quote brief excerpts for review is granted without further permission when accompanied by publication data.

Except where otherwise indicated, all Scripture quotations in this book are taken from the Holy Bible, New International Version®, NIV®. Copyright ©1973, 1978, 1984, 2011 by Biblica, Inc.™ Used by permission of Zondervan. All rights reserved worldwide. www.zondervan.com The "NIV" and "New International Version" are trademarks registered in the United States Patent and Trademark Office by Biblica, Inc.™

Disclaimer: This work depicts actual events in the life of the author as truthfully as recollection permits and/or can be verified by research. All persons within are actual individuals; there are no composite characters. Some names and identifying details have been changed to protect the privacy of individuals.

Front cover image by T.J. Liqeur.
Front cover designer by M. H. Pasindu Lakshan.

FIRST EDITION

LivingLifeFullyAlive.com

For more information, please contact the author at the following email address: Sealed4LifeByChrist@gmail.com.

ISBN 978-0-578-66051-6 (Paperback)

I dedicate this book to my Lord and Savior, Jesus Christ, the author and finisher of my life story.

I will repay you for the years the locusts have eaten— the great locust and the young locust, the other locusts and the locust swarm— my great army that I sent among you.

Joel 2:25

Preface

When I was a young girl, I prayed for a powerful testimony. Well, I certainly got one. Now it's finally time to share a part of that with you.

Years ago, I began writing this memoir after God put it on my heart. I put it down, I picked it up…. and that cycle repeated until I finally heeded the voice of the Lord, nudging me on a still Christmas night— a night God arranged so I could simply sit quietly with Him and finish the task He had been urging me to complete. Frankly speaking, I had been running.

This book is a recollection of events in my life that took place over ten years ago; a bit of the good times, a bit of the rough times, and bits of everything in between. Most importantly, it's an account of insights gleaned in retrospect when I spent intimate moments with the Lord.

During these quiet times of resting in God's presence, I took off the mask I had put on and truly examined my heart to see how and when the enemy had attempted to come in and steal my purpose, dating back to my youngest years up until my late twenties. As I sorted through what seemed like a mess, the Lord showed me where He was present in every circumstance— the good, the bad, and the ugly. He spoke to me in those moments. And in that stillness, He showed me the truth about where He was and what He had been trying to tell me during the moments when I was not willing or "available" to seek His presence.

The end result? Clarity. Healing at the deepest of levels. Call it a purifying and cleansing process if you will. Did it hurt at times to bear my soul to the Lord?

Yes! Salt water certainly stings when it touches an unhealed wound; however, if a wound goes unattended, it festers—and festering wounds remain unhealed. During this process of healing very deep wounds, I found peace with my past, and I saw that the Lord had always been moving in my life, even in the moments when I did not want to live. It seems like a lifetime ago that I felt this way, but God has a wonderful way of taking what is broken and transforming it into something new.

I consider the chapters of my life story documented here a memoir of remembrance—of gratitude—of worship—of praise—praise that I simply am alive in Christ and confident that He holds the whole world in His hands. I am so grateful the Lord used this process to cleanse me at the deepest level from all past trauma, for giving me another chance at life, and for asking me if I was willing to share this part of my story with you. For this, I am beyond honored.

~Lyndsay Wrensen

Introduction

I have seen all the "colors of the ocean" in my lifetime thus far—from the clear light blue ripples near the surface—to the deep and darker blue waters away from the shore, as God relentlessly took me into the depths of the sea as He drew me closer to Him. Despite the "waves of life" I have faced and may face again along the journey of life, I consider myself blessed beyond measure.

I believe that when we are willing to allow those waves of life to move us to a new level of trust and healing, we become stronger and ready for the next step that God has already prepared for us to accomplish with His power in His perfect time.

These chapters of the "book of my life" summarize what I had, what I once considered a loss, and what I now see as a precious gift—a miracle in the making—the gift of wisdom and God's amazing grace, mercy, and sovereignty—a true example of His restoration and redemption.

Nothing was ever lost. In fact, what I gained during the time of my life captured within the pages of this book I consider invaluable and irreplaceable. It's not the things of the world that I consider most valuable today; it is the beauty and love I've discovered as I've made it past shallow waters and learned to walk with the Lord along my journey of faith.

You may find some of what I mention in this book explicit. I even include some journal entries that might be hard to hear. However, in recollecting these memories with gratitude, God showed me more than just a glimpse of His amazing grace, and He used each trial to turn me into an overcomer. He took the old and made it new. He took the broken pieces of my life and weaved them into a beautiful patchwork quilt as He lined me up with His true purpose and calling in my life. And all I had to do was surrender to His will; surrender often at times, which will always be a daily process.

This is the story of the first twenty-something years of my life, the tough lessons learned, and how God never left my side. He allowed me to become broken to the point of needing complete restoration. I was, simply put, as somebody once said, "a beautiful mess." But as poised and perfect as I tried to appear behind my mask, I was living a double life. Yes, my life includes many high points at first. That is, until that double line blurred into one set of lines. *The wrong path.*

However, God knew my purpose and saw me through His loving eyes. When He intervened, He miraculously guided me back to my path of destiny. He had always been there, extending His loving hand to me. Once I accepted it, He propelled me over each wave I faced, one step at a time.

Contents

Chapter One: Still Waters

Start children off on the way they should go,
and even when they are old they will not turn from it.
~Proverbs 22:9

I was born one fall morning in upstate New York to two loving parents who were determined to provide all that was needed for me to be all I was created to be.

I immediately became the apple of my parents' eyes. My home life was happy and fulfilling. I was placed into a Godly home, where I received constant love and security from my devoted and adoring parents. I became daddy's little girl and my mother's first born of her two blue-eyed little girls.

My mother had met my father while he was lifeguarding on the sandy shores of Jones Beach in Long Island, New York. Her home was also New York. Although she had a teaching degree, she made a living as a first-class flight attendant with United Airlines.

My mother has one of the most beautiful hearts of anyone I have ever met; she is full of life and love. All those around her seem to notice it. She grew up in a wealthy household, yet her father was often abusive to her, her siblings, and his wife, my grandmother. He was a successful businessman in New York who knew exactly how to get what he wanted.

I never saw the darker side of him; his heart softened more so in his later years after my birth. My mother once reminded me that he accepted Christ into his heart while my sister and I sat on his lap telling him of our love for Jesus. I have fond memories of him.

My mother's experiences with her father during her childhood fueled her determination to provide an enhanced and healthier life for her own family; thus, she demonstrated and enforced Christian values in our household. She was certainly an example of how to live like Christ.

After facing a critical health struggle prior to meeting my father, my mother had turned her life over to Christ, as had her sister, mother, and my great-grandmother. My mother only allowed Godly people and things into our home, including music and television shows; anything that was not of Christ did not enter through the door. God was the head of the household, and I loved every moment of the protected joyful life that came with this.

I also had an amazing role model as a father, who has such a caring heart and protective nature. I respect and admire his motivation, intelligence, discernment, diligence, and strong reasoning skills. He used these skills to pursue a career in psychology. I was very close with my father as a child, and I still am today.

As an infant, my father served as both mom and dad when my mother was traveling for work. When I was a very young child, he was open to my inclination to create adventures and games both indoors and outside, although I naturally gravitated to being outdoors. Using various toys as well as things one would find in nature, we would build obstacle courses together in our backyard, calling it "Candy Land," named after my favorite board game. We made sure that the last stop was under my favorite tree, where I loved to read and write by myself, singing joyfully while I scribbled and colored amongst the stacks of books to my left and right. My father always went above and beyond to do special things for me, such as building me a beautiful doll house as well as a playhouse in our backyard. He inspired me to pursue my dreams. I remember him saying, "If you can dream it, you can achieve it." He was right. I have big dreams, and certainly believe in the power of God to move on my behalf and instruct me to fulfill them, although they may seem lofty to some.

A dreamer and believer, my life was amazing. Even the sky was not a limit. I was a visionary from the start, with very bold, vibrant dreams that influenced my expression through writing, singing, dance, art, and other creative outlets. I was an energetic and animated child who liked to keep busy and entertained, yet I was innovative and independent when not playing with others. Playful and bold, I had a vivid imagination that knew no limits. It went anywhere. It did anything.

Life became more enlivening when I had a new playmate, my younger sister, who was born before I turned three. As a natural leader, I was excited to step into this role of being a big sis—and she loved being just like her big sis.

Although I loved my younger sister, I did not like the loss of my parents' undivided attention, as I was used to having the spotlight. I certainly was bossy and demanding toward my younger sister at times, although my motive was based in love. She was very gentle and easy-going, and I wanted to show her all the interesting things I had discovered, hoping she too would join me in my creative exploration. I wanted to teach her. I enjoyed telling her all the rules of the games I dreamed up for us to play, as I was passionate about all I created. I wanted her to share this excitement.

I wrote skits and songs for us to perform for my parents in front of our fireplace. I taught her ballet in the kitchen that I learned from my dance classes. I served as the teacher when we played school on the deck. I made her my student in *all* that I did. We have some hilarious home videos singing and dancing together to old Amy Grant songs, using spatulas as microphones! *(Side note: I sometimes still use that same spatula from the 80's while rehearsing!)*

Although my little sis admired her big sis and we had fun together, looking back now, I see I was domineering and had a need for control. I didn't understand when she wouldn't focus on things *I* saw as very important, such as music and dance. She was quite comfortable simply relaxing with my mother. Me, on the other hand? I could rarely sit still.

When she did not want to participate in my productions, I learned to be quite content alone. I loved to write at a young age. When I looked back at the many notebooks filled with stories, plays, and songs later in life, I was honestly impressed. Little did I know I would need them down the road to remember who I was after I lost my way. Looking back at these notebooks was one way the Lord reminded me of my identity in Christ.

Ah, that childlike spirit. I truly had a sense of wonder.

Much of my writing was done in my quiet time with God, which I loved. I was peaceful and serene writing and singing one-on-one with Jesus. I had accepted Jesus Christ as my Savior at a young age, and I developed a very personal relationship with Him. This relationship inspired my writing and singing.

I believe the closer we are to Christ, the closer we are to our *true* destiny—the dreams that God placed in our heart before we were born. Every gift He births in us is made to be used for His glory. As a child, He caused these gifts to stir up inside of me for the right reasons and seasons. However, life can cause us to forget those passions, and the enemy can certainly attempt to use them for his plans. I am so thankful that the Lord brought my passions to life and continues to protect me and guide me so that my gifts are used for His purposes.

Yes, I knew Jesus at an intimate level as a very young child, which would not have been the case without my loving parents, who were both believers. My mother had a fervor and passion for Christ that naturally overflowed onto me. I was provided a strong foundation in the Word at home, and I found rest in the secret place in my quiet time with God. I loved Jesus, and I loved others. I believed everything the Word of God stated. I absolutely felt free. As my parents surrounded themselves with positive people and only wanted the best for me, they also placed me in Christian school and church where I was surrounded by those same values and other children who were raised in faith. I knew nothing other than God's love. I was very protected. I had no fear, no worries, and I felt completely safe and free to be myself and live my dreams.

One of my biggest dreams as a little girl was to be on what I called "Christian Broadway." This was inspired by watching a very young actress and singer who performed on my favorite Christian music television show which aired on Saturday mornings.

Music and theatrical performances played a huge role in my life from the start. I loved to spontaneously sing and dance around the house and outside in our large backyard. Singing was my passion. I look back now and realize what I was doing was prophetically praising and worshiping God all day long. The words The Lord gave me were overflowing from my heart to my mouth. Even when I did my chores on Saturday mornings, I sang, danced, and turned it into a game. *(Side note: I still do this today. In fact, I love to clean!)*

Music also played a role in terms of spiritual warfare at a very young age. I believe one of the biggest impacts upon my life that set up a strong foundation for fighting in the spirit was a children's song I was taught in church in which we commanded the enemy to flee in the name of Jesus Christ, claiming that we have victory as believers in Him. If I remember correctly, these powerful lyrics stated: "I command you, Satan, in the name of the Lord, to take up your weapons and flee! For the Lord has given me authority to stomp all over thee!" As children, we loved to sing this song while literally stomping on the ground and telling Satan to flee. I often did this in my prayer closet. I took it seriously. I will forever be thankful for those leaders in that children's ministry for teaching me that song, because that mindset of declaring victory over the enemy was implanted within my heart from that point forward.

Victory is the anthem of my life; regardless of the intensity of the battle or if I am the target of attack. I know the battle has already been won, and I am on the winning side, right next to the King of Kings!

Walking with the Lord and being in the secure and protected environment of my loving and watchful parents, however, was not necessarily the reality of the outside world. For example, inside my home, we were not exposed to secular music or television. I was quite trusting, because I had trustworthy people all around me.

The Lord used a trial at the age of four or five to prepare me for the ways of the world when I encountered something did not line up with the

Christian behaviors exhibited by my parents. The words and actions of an extended family member startled and confused me having never been exposed to something of that nature. These memories are vague given that I was young, yet it resulted in confusion of sexuality and subsequent feelings of guilt and shame that I carried with me for many years. The memory I repressed did not surface until my late twenties. It took a lot of digging to heal from these wounds. Looking back in retrospect, I see it altered my perception of love for many years.

I have learned that all lessons in life our vital to our calling. As protected and secure as I was, the Lord used it to show me the world would not always be my friend, but He could carry me through anything in life. There was much more that I would encounter intended to harm me. He wanted me to learn to trust Him as my best friend, my loving Father, and my healer. He wanted me to learn how He watches over me and will not let the enemy win. After forgiveness and healing, I see now the Lord used all of that as preparation. I am thankful for those experiences, as I developed true empathy for others I would later encounter.

We may not always understand a situation in the moment, but with God as our director, He sheds light on those valuable lessons just when we need them! He knew I would not be able to confront what I later faced without allowing this, and He wanted me to have true understanding, compassion, and empathy when ministering to others. I am grateful today for this. It enabled me to be used by God to bring healing to others later in life, as He healed me! The Lord knew I was willing to be used, because He knows my heart and faith in Him as my Savior.

—————————————————————

Just as I was learning to trust in Christ, my father was trusting God about a move our family would soon make. When I was six-years old, my parents called us in for a family meeting. A major door had opened in Atlanta for my father to lead a large project for the Georgia State Department of Mental Health. Although he viewed it as risky as he had an amazing job in New York and was set up for success there, my father felt it was a good move for the family. Given my mother's parents had relocated to the area years before, she was naturally thrilled and highly supportive of the move. My father had not expected such an amazing opportunity to open in Atlanta where my mother's parents had moved, so this was a huge blessing for our family.

Being so young, my main concern was leaving the New York snow and my huge backyard where I loved to play and could freely express myself without being told to be quiet! With my high-energy level, I was never content sitting still doing anything that I did not feel was meaningful, inspiring, and supportive to my well-being and creative flow. Thus, the backyard was my playground, where I could play without being ordered around by others. I could live and play in my fairy-tale adventures alone with Christ, where I felt so free.

However, I loved my grandma and papa in Atlanta, as well as the pool at their home, where my father had taught me to swim as a very young child. I loved to swim, so I looked forward to this.

Soon enough, we relocated to a beautiful upper-middle class suburban neighborhood in a wealthy county just outside of Atlanta where my father worked. My sister and I were placed in a large well-known and well-established private Christian school that we attended for seven years.

I wasn't the most popular kid in school, but I had an amazing group of close friends, although I was very shy. I see now that I was more of a leader than a follower, as I did not want to participate in breaking the rules. I was focused and quiet at school and loved to learn. Any interruption to my ability to learn from others was quite frustrating to me. Even at this young age, I craved knowledge and was mainly concerned with learning and achieving my personal goals and dreams. I chose friends with the same mindsets.

From what I have heard from others, including my mother, who is still close friends with many of my teachers during these years, the teachers loved me, and I was viewed as the picture-perfect student. On several occasions, I won the "Timothy Award" for the "Most Christ-like attitude." Year after year, I was one of the few students that received the "Perfect Attendance Award," and I was not happy if I did not receive an A+ on an assignment. To this day, my mother still jokes that I asked for more homework on a semi-frequent basis. She noted to me that she recalls the joy she felt when her friends would call me the "perfect-child." However, she also would get frustrated when I would not go to sleep because I was focused on reading and creating. If anything, she had to tell me to stop doing my homework.

Apart from my academics, which I excelled in, I was known for singing songs during chapel at school on stage by myself. Performing on stage came very natural to me. I started taking voice-lessons in fourth grade, and I loved performing in chapel, recitals, school musicals, and chorus. I continued with dance as well. I did not care about popularity or being front and center unless it related to what I truly loved— music. That was my passion, and I felt very comfortable on stage if I was singing to glorify the Lord.

I remember I had an appearance on an Evangelist's Television show. They came to my house in Atlanta to interview me for a ten-minute segment about my love for and faith in Christ, my ability to speak in tongues, the fact I saw spiritual warfare as vital at a young age, and how I spoke life over myself and rebuked the devil from harming me amid a class full of students with chicken pox. I was fearful about diseases and sickness, but I did not tell the network this. Because of this fear, I handled it in my prayer closet. I was honest and bold about my faith in Christ, speaking about the outcome of the devil boldly. *By the way, I did not get the chicken pox that year!*

Anything that I did as a child, I did for the Lord. I was in a children's Christian dancing and singing group called "Just Jammin' for Jesus" in sixth grade. We practiced often and performed at homeless shelters and nursing homes. It was run by an amazing woman of God and mother of one of my girlfriends at school who also loved to sing and dance.

In addition to going to the same Christian private school from second to seventh grade, it was also our church home, and in fifth grade, it became the employer of both my mother and father. My mother substitute taught at our school when I was young. My sister and I very much enjoyed having our mother nearby at school; in fact, we knew nothing other than this. My mother was later offered a teaching position at the school. My sixth-grade Math and Bible teacher was none other than my own beautiful mother, and her closest friends were many of the teachers I had over the years. The prayers of these amazing women of God have carried me through some of the darkest times in my life, and I am so grateful for them. My mother is still very close with them, and I get to see and speak to them often. I truly love this special group of ladies. They are dear to me.

When we did not ride with my mother to school, we often rode with my father, who was offered a position within the school after he transitioned from a career in clinical psychology to school psychology. At a young age, I was very interested in the work my father did. I would often ask him about his job, yet he was very clear he could not give me the details about my peers. He took his position very seriously, and I highly respected him. I saw his role as very interesting and valuable, and I began to develop a passion for psychology.

Although a year younger than most of my peers as I had started school earlier than my classmates, I was spiritually, emotionally, and mentally very mature. Like my father, I was an intellectual. I found most of the conversation with many of my peers to lack true substance. I was not interested in being popular, because I saw much of what came with it as immature and lacking valuable substance. I was focused on being all that I could be.

Sounds picture perfect, right?

━━━━━━━━━━━━━━━━━━━━━━━━━━━━

*What a beautiful thing, when you are so secure in who you are in Christ, that you feel free to be all you were made to be, regardless of what others are doing or what they might think. What a beautiful thing, when you can be the **unique one-of-a-kind** person you were **designed** to be without doubt trying to influence you to conform to the ways of the world or strip you from the **uniqueness** placed within you for your unique **one-of-a-kind** calling. Conforming to the ways of the world is a plot of the enemy to keep you from your destiny, an attempt to leave you with emptiness, regret, bitterness, loneliness, and a lack of the fulfillment that can be found in being all you were created to be! What a beautiful thing, when you can peacefully and joyfully be in the world, but not of it, marching towards your ultimate purpose, hand-in-hand with Jesus Christ, the living water for the salt of the Earth, who brings us to still waters when we trust in Him. What a beautiful thing, when we raise up our children to know their true purpose is found in Christ alone.*

━━━━━━━━━━━━━━━━━━━━━━━━━━━━

Chapter Two: Standing Waves and the Change of Tides

Be on your guard; stand firm in the faith; be courageous;
be strong.
~1 Corinthians 16:13

During those first twelve years of my life, I remained pure, strong in the Lord, and focused on what I felt held true significance. However, even in a Christian school, I somehow felt ridiculed by other students for being so devoted to Christ and being "different." This may have been a lie of the enemy, but it was my perception at the time. I began to feel like an outsider, so I tried to hide my light by hiding myself. That was a trick from the enemy that does not work on me today! I am proud to be unique. I am proud to be bold, and I am proud to let my light shine bright like a star for Him. God made me who I am for His perfect plan for His Kingdom.

Although I was extremely shy at school, I was very animated at home where I felt free to be myself. In addition to voice and dance lessons, I took horseback riding, swimming, piano, and figure skating lessons. My mother loved horses, and my father had played minor league hockey prior to meeting my mother, hence my desire to figure skate. Thus, I had similar interests to both of my parents.

I loved dressing up, makeup, and simply being a "girly-girl." Unlike my mother, I was drawn to pageantry, modeling, and acting; activities she saw as risky and worldly. I urged her to allow me to enter pageants, but she resisted my pleas. I saw these activities as unique—a creative outlet—a form of art and expression. I was a twelve-year-old going on 22. I loved expressing myself by coordinating unique outfits, putting together fashion shows with friends and family members, setting up photoshoots with backdrops and props and urging my sister to be my model, and doing my own "commercials" on our video camera. Eventually, my parents allowed me to take modeling and acting classes and enter a pageant.

Although I was independent and content on my own, as I grew older, the importance of having a social life weighed on me. I craved diversity outside of the group of friends I had gone to school with for six years, and I figured public school might have more opportunities in terms of new friendships, activities, clubs, and leadership positions. I wanted to see the world. I wanted a challenge. Today, I know I feel most satisfied when living outside of the "box." I think sometimes we place God in a box, but He is so creative, and He is always new. *Like Father, like daughter!*

Before my last year of middle school, my parents decided to leave our private school after leadership changes, and they enrolled my sister and me in public school, hoping that we would not be influenced in a negative way. My mother had once seen public education as "the big bad wolf" that would lead her children astray. Today, I know that regardless of where we are, it is up to us as individuals to remain faithful to Christ as believers.

I was excited to venture into new territory, especially as a new neighborhood girlfriend was going to be entering the school with me, although she would be in the grade below mine. She was new to the area and my first close girlfriend outside of Christian school and church. Furthermore, another girlfriend from private school would also be joining me at our new school as we lived in the same district. I was excited that we could do it together, yet I had no idea what to expect.

Eighth grade was a very challenging year. I was still learning to make friends for the first time outside all I had known up until that point. I was a very recognizable "goody-goody." The school and students were very different from private school. Many of the boys had long hair and wore saggy pants as opposed to the strict dress code and clean-cut appearance required at private school. Several of the girls wore tight fitting baby T's with suggestive imagery and verbiage. This may have been a trend of the time, but it was quite different from what I knew. I was considered the preppy girl from private school.

I was shocked when the boys so freely approached me on my first day of school. At first, it made me uncomfortable. I was not used to this. Perhaps this was because my parents had worked at my private school and everyone was aware of it. I also did not want to get in trouble by chatting when we were supposed to be paying attention to the teacher. Yes, I was undeniably a teacher's pet.

I was very serious and focused on school, although I did not always feel academically challenged. I started to get anxiety when the teachers were not going at the pace I desired. It frustrated me, and many of the other students did not stay focused as we were instructed to do in private school. Classes there had been smaller and more structured. Here, it seemed there was a higher level of tolerance for disorderly behavior. I often thought to myself, "We are here to learn, why do others feel led to get approval from classmates by disobeying?" I tried to ignore it, but it annoyed me.

Remaining quiet and meek, I excelled academically. Mentally, I began preparing myself for a leadership position with student council in high school. In my chorus class, I felt confident and was a leader. My other classes seemed so simple and by the book at times. Getting my school work done was my priority so that I could have time at home to be creative.

In chorus class, I loved getting the solos, and I tried out for All-State Chorus and missed the acceptance criteria cut-off by a mere half of a point, although I was praised for coming so close as an eighth grader. This became another goal for my first year of high school.

There was one student in my chorus class that did not seem to notice my talent in singing. To be more transparent, he did not notice *me*. He did appear to notice the girls around him though! I was a first soprano and sat far away from him in the classroom, but I thought perhaps he would notice my talent and eventually notice *me*. I perceived him not noticing me as rejection. I did not have the chance to get to know him, and it frustrated me, but I was not going to get out of line and risk getting in trouble to grab his attention. Never. But the main reason? I was overly shy. I decided to let it go, still being hopeful that one day I would have the chance to get to know him.

He had a bad boy image, per my perception, yet I was drawn to him. I was curious and intrigued by those who seemed lost. *He* seemed lost. I wanted to help him find his way. I wanted to know *more*. I wanted to know *why*.

I remember being in gym class one day when I noticed him walking alone near the gym doors, although he was not in my PE class. I wondered why he appeared to be...wandering. I felt empathy for him, although I did not know why he was not in his own class, so I assumed he was skipping.

At that moment, I truly heard God's voice in my heart, asking me to pray for him specifically. So, I did. In fact, I have never stopped praying for him.

I asked my girlfriend from private school about him, as I knew he was on her eighth-grade team and she was a part of the popular crowd like him. Although I cannot remember now how she responded, she asked me to join her at a party one student was having where I thought I might be able to meet him. Although I was hesitant to go to a party with the popular crowd, I accepted her invitation.

When we got to the party, I remember seeing him there. I did not want to approach him without being introduced, but I walked with a group of girls to get on a trampoline where he was sitting alone. I curiously watched as he conversed with the others. I remained quiet but friendly and open to conversation. He seemed less coherent than normal. He was smiling and happy, but not keeping himself together. As the others started to walk away, I decided that this was my one chance to be alone and talk with him. I had to brake past my bashfulness. I stayed there with him, fighting my timidity. He never saw me at school. Maybe he would tonight.

But he did not "see me," although we did have a brief conversation. He took a sip of the drink in his hand, looked at me, then asked if I wanted some. I told him no, wondering why he offered me something to drink. I was curious what was making him so comfortable talking to me now? Never having spoken to someone my age or thereabouts who had been drinking, I did not understand why he was acting so different than he did at school. I assumed after the party he would speak to me at school, but I had no idea that alcohol can lead to memory loss.

I learned about alcohol causing memory loss first-hand years later. Many people "met" a former version of me during those years, yet I did not "meet" them. In fact, after years of severe addiction in my twenties, I did not remember much of my life in general until I got still after numerous hardships that allowed God to draw me back to His will. It can be hard to make the right decisions when things are blocking your view. I had to clear out the rear-view mirror, go back to certain memories, be still, and listen for revelation.

I walked away, realizing I had no idea where my friend had gone. It was pitch black outside. I began to feel extreme social anxiety as I searched for her amongst the strangers stumbling around the backyard. I was not used to social situations like this.

Finally, I saw someone I recognized from school, and I asked him if he had seen my girlfriend. He told me he had not and offered me a cigarette. I was anxious and did not know what to do with myself, so I accepted the cigarette.

I was not listening to God at that moment, despite His reasoning with me to say no. I was being a follower of the popular crowd rather than a leader. I felt shame and disgust after I smoked, so I ran to call my mother to pick me up from the party. When she arrived, I sat in the backseat of her mini-van and kept my mouth shut. I was filled with guilt for smoking.

After that day, I felt pressured to sin...to conform...to follow the crowd...to go after the bad boys who did not allow me close to them. The grass ended up not being greener on the other side. Years later, I realized I had given in to the enemy and followed the ways of the world in my attempts to understand the "lost."

The popular way of the world is not necessarily the right way. Following Christ, however, leads to the most valuable reward.

I found myself in similar environments over time, as we all face pressure to conform to the world. I was introduced to another boy at our school. Although I had zero interested in him, I felt pressured when my best girlfriend suggested I "go out" with him, so I did. I didn't want to, but I felt like this is what everyone was doing. This decision left me with an unsettling feeling. One night, my parents let me go to his house, which was quite different from my life at home. I was nervous and hesitant to go in the first place, and I felt very uncomfortable when I was asked if I was a virgin and attempts were made to influence me to "be easy" once I arrived. I was overwhelmed; I hadn't even had my first kiss! I did not consider his requests because I knew it was not right and simply didn't want that. I had no desire to give in to the pressure. This was not an area of temptation for me. My heart was beating fast, screaming "leave!" At that point, I called my parents to pick me up immediately.

However, when I was around my girlfriends, I had a harder time resisting other temptations. I tried marijuana with my best girlfriend, the boy I was "going out" with, and a few other eighth-graders one day after school while I was at her house. I was extremely anxious and never felt the effect of the drug. I kept my eye on the time, eager for my mother to arrive. I resisted calling her to pick me up early this time as to not embarrass myself, but I felt my anxiety level rising with every moment. I wanted out of the situation.

Another evening at my house, I gave in to my best friend's request to allow the same boy and his friend to come over. My parents would never have allowed this. When they arrived, I stood firm in my convictions, remained on good behavior, and attempted to influence the others to do the same. I felt a loss of control as this did not happen. My younger sister was also home and confused as to why friends were in my room without me. I cleaned up a mess as quickly as possible and told them my parents would be coming home early. I anxiously waited for the boys to leave.

After this event, I distanced myself from this group of kids, including my best friend at the time (who is a strong woman of faith today and a friend I am very grateful for) and the boy I was no longer "going out with." However, I found myself influenced by the actions of those who lived nearby my house and rode my school bus.

More temptations to sin! It seemed I could not get away from it.

This time, I was influenced by the words of my close neighborhood girlfriend who had become tight with some of the kids on the bus. Several of them decided to smoke cigarettes in the woods in our neighborhood near a construction site as the developers were expanding our neighborhood. My girlfriend grabbed some of her grandmother's cigarettes, and I joined her and the others in the woods one day after school. I don't think I inhaled any of the times I joined in on this activity at thirteen years old, yet we continued with sneaking cigarettes here and there. We got away with it every time, and I began to have less anxiety when I was rebellious. Lying became much easier.

Weeks later, my eleven-year-old sister began to wonder what I was doing and asked if she could try it, although I don't think she truly wanted to nor did she think *trying it* was even a possibility. I rode my bike to one of the neighborhood kid's homes looking for a cigarette *on my own*. This time, no close girlfriend influenced me to do this. I had become a *follower* of the crowd, and I was literally *leading* my sister to wander with me into the "forest" (i.e., the construction area within our neighborhood amongst the trees).

In hiding. In secret. But all darkness eventually comes to light.

After spraying cheap body splash and changing my shirt, I walked back into the house and sat down for dinner with my family. Suddenly, my sister blurted out that I had been smoking. I lied, and I got away with it. The moment I told that lie, I was deceived that lies work.

Decisions today certainly shape our world tomorrow. It took many years for the deceit to catch up with me, but when it did, it served a purpose. I eventually learned that lies do not work. They do not; no matter how you look at it. God always brings the truth to light. You cannot trick God, and He does not like seeing His

23

children deceived by others with no remorse! No matter how far ahead of God we try to go by deceiving others, God will bring us to a place where we see that love is not lies. He only wants the best for us, and we must allow Him to teach us for our own benefit. It is always for our good. His plans are exceedingly above and beyond our expectations, but the devil tries to convince us that there will be a negative result if we do not take an easy out.

We are always given a choice. Our choices do matter. Every single choice we make matters. When we fail to trust in God's direction and respond in action by making the wrong choices, we must face any consequences.

Later that school year, I smoked another cigarette at a high school football game. I had tried it several times; what would another time hurt given I had always gotten away with it in the woods in my neighborhood?

A friend and I were the only two students caught amongst the massive group of eight-graders that night. My father did not believe the security officer when he called to tell him *his* daughter had been caught smoking. In fact, my teachers were also questioning why I would have done this, and they lessened my penalty after my mother called an administrator. She was beside herself, and my father was still in disbelief about my behavior. It just did not seem to make sense. As far as me, I did not feel better about myself after this. I felt worse.

I had chosen to follow the crowd because I was deceived that it was fun—that I would be accepted.

24

My parents responded by grounding me, which kept me out of further harm's way. I am so thankful for that today, although the right way is not always fun in the moment! This was not the last time the Lord protected me in a similar way.

Today, looking back, I know now why God tells us to be grateful in all circumstances. In this case and many others, being reprimanded was for my own protection and growth. Thankfully, God had a way of leading me back on the right path, regardless of where I had risked going that year, and I chose to surrender to His plan. I got back on the right path.

What a beautiful thing, when we love our children by disciplining them, just as the Lord does for us! The seasons change; the tides also change, but God's love never fails. What a beautiful thing, when young children are protected by instruction and discipline from loving and forgiving parents, who impart to their children leadership and wisdom to pass to future generations. We must remember that love is patient, and what may not understand in the moment, God has already intended for a beautiful purpose.

Chapter Three: Breakwater

*We all, like sheep, have gone astray, each of us has
turned to our own way; and the LORD has laid on him the
iniquity of us all.*
~Isaiah 53:6

My mother's voice echoed loud in my head along with
the illustration she often drew on paper. I wanted to
stay *in* God's circle instead of *out* of it.

When I was young, my mother would draw a circle
with the word "God" written inside the circle and the
words "sex," "drugs," and "alcohol" outside the circle.
That is the mindset I had been carrying for years and
carried with me as I entered my first year of high
school at age 13, a year younger than my peers. I was
determined to do everything right in high school.

Although I would have to part ways with many of the
friends I had made in middle school and make new
friends again as many of them were in another high
school district, perhaps this was a good thing. I
certainly had not always chosen friends wisely in new
environments. I was very naive and overly trusting.

The only students I knew at my new high school were
those who lived within my neighborhood, which was
stereotyped as the rich kids' subdivision. I was not
close with many of those students where I lived, but I
was comforted in knowing a female family friend from
New York who had been like a sister to me in my
younger years was entering her second year at my
new high school.

On the first day of school, she took me under her wing,
and I sat with her and her friends during lunch. She
seemed to have an amazing group of friends, most of

whom were actively involved in leadership positions within student council as well as other clubs, sports, and various activities. Again, that fueled the spark that had ignited in middle school to be a part of student council, yet I remained extremely shy and had yet to come out of my shell.

Although I excelled in my classes, I did not like raising my hand, despite the fact I knew the answers. This was nothing new. If I was called on, I could feel my face immediately grow warm as I began to blush. In my mind, it was bright red and apparent to everyone. However, I enjoyed social interaction in small groups, and I had gained some confidence in my ability to make friends the prior year. I honestly cannot think of a single person whom I did not get along with; I liked the diversity at the school. Finding the right core group of friends to sit with during lunch and get together with on the weekends, however, was a priority. I naturally gravitated towards wanting to hang with the popular crowd.

My new best friend was likely the most well-liked girl in my class of over 900 freshmen students, but she was also humble, intelligent, extremely sweet and bubbly, and a strong Christian. In middle school, my perception of the popular group was that they were mostly the kids who tended to get in trouble. This was not the case with my best friend. She was a cheerleader and seen as a leader in our freshmen class. We hung in the same circle of friends, but it was often just the two of us on the weekends. I'm sure we were considered "Christian goody-goodies," but she was so fun and full of life that I had no reason to feel like an outsider because of my faith. We had a blast together, and I joined her church, where I met more amazing people.

I also got very involved in my school following her lead. She decided to run for class President, and I ran for Vice-President, which meant we would be our class leaders along with another amazing Christian girl. It was a wonderful experience that continued all four years of high school. In fact, I was later elected as a member of the Executive Board of Student Council. Although I was shy, I was well-respected by my peers, teachers, and the administrators of my school.

I joined as many other clubs, honors societies, and activities as possible in addition to my Advanced Placement and honors classes, chorus involvement, voice-lessons, and figure-skating lessons. I excelled in my advanced chorus class and made All-State Chorus after coming very close the previous year. Most of my girlfriends were cheerleaders, so I was very involved with football games on Friday nights as well as all the prep work with the Pep Rally Club before the games. Afterwards, we often got together for dinner or went to spend the night at a girlfriends' house. I was not interested in dating the first two years of high school. I was more focused on school, activities, and my close girlfriends.

However, one Friday night, I caught sight of someone of interest. That evening, I had hesitantly accepted my parents offer to eat Mexican at their typical go-to spot. I hated Mexican food at the time, but given I was hungry and had no other plans, I decided to go. At that age, I did not want to be seen with my parents, especially on a Friday night.

After we ate our dinner, I grew impatient and could not sit still while they conversed, which was the norm. I asked my mother for a quarter and walked to the front of the restaurant to play a video game. Right before I inserted the coin into an old Pac Man game, I froze. Talking to the kitchen staff near the kitchen was that boy from my eighth-grade chorus class who I had chatted with on the trampoline at my first "real" party!

I could feel my face turning beet red, so I surveyed the room for a quick escape so he would not see me. Instead, I darted outside and took a loop to my parents' locked car. I thought to myself, "Should I go back in? Will I have the courage to talk to him? But maybe he's up to no good? Maybe he's dealing drugs. Okay…I should stay away…No, I should be confident and approach him."

When I went back inside, I didn't see him, so I walked back to our table inside the restaurant. Perhaps the next time my parents asked me to grab Mexican on a Friday night, I would go without complaints in hopes of seeing him. Maybe I would be prepared to confidently approach him by then. I was more than curious. But I never saw him again until many years later. *(Side note: I will not share that part of my story now, but I will say God used this person in a powerful life-changing way many years down the road!)*

As the seasons came and gone, I had not yet dated, nor had I even had my first "real" kiss. I was very innocent and terrified that if I somehow "did it" wrong, it would be the end of the world.

I decided to work that summer as a lifeguard at a water amusement park. It was a perfect job for me, and I met a pretty, fun, smart and savvy new girlfriend who became one of my closest friends that summer. We are still connected, and I have wonderful memories of the times we spent together. She was very outgoing and went to another school in the county. She loved my sense of humor, which I never

30

thought was so humorous. But I over time, I realized it was unique, and I grew to like it as well. I began to enjoy being the source of entertainment outside of my home life. I felt I could be myself. She allowed me to be as goofy as I wanted, a side I rarely let anyone see. Our friendship boosted my confidence in many ways.

That was the summer I finally came out of my shell. However, when I came out of my "shell," I also started venturing further out of "God's circle." My eyes began to see a lot more than I had been exposed to previously, and I started participating in things I knew I should not be doing.

This summer began my very slow progression towards sleepwalking in the land of the lost—the beginning of being trapped in various forms of bondage; a strenuous detour that preceded my journey of rediscovering the access point to the "right path." Fortunately, I serve a God who loves me with such an everlasting love that He saved me from myself. It is truly a miracle that I am alive today.

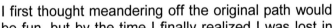

I first thought meandering off the original path would be fun, but by the time I finally realized I was lost in the forest, I looked around only to see that most everyone had seemed to move on from that dark place except for me. And the others? Many are no longer alive.

It is never fun to be left alone in the dark. Where did I go wrong? Well, I followed the crowd—the popular way. I started to ignore the guidance of my Heavenly Father. I played hide and seek with God, venturing in and out of that dimly lit lane for many years, although He saw me the whole time and refused to let me go.

I did what I wanted, when I wanted, and my love for God began to hide inside of the darkness I was allowing into my life. But I had no idea, because I was blinded by the false lights that distracted me from the true wisdom from above which kept knocking on my heart, telling me to stop and take a U-turn! I was headed down a path of destruction, and I ignored all the subtle road signs telling me that this was a detour. It *looked* like the right way, but I was slowly meandering out of God's will. I did not see this for many years until it was completely obvious that I would die if I did not turn around and run back into the arms of The Lord.

The hardest part? Accepting that I had made a series of wrong-turns and had to face the consequences. There were no barriers making the initial deviations, but there sure seemed to be mountain in the way as I returned to Him! However, God is The Mountain Mover. Faith can move mountains. I am so thankful for those who were interceding on my behalf.

That being said, let's get back to the story of how this happened…

I was loving my slow induction into the ways of the world. Tipsy nights of drinking with friends from work turned into hangovers and lies to my parents. I remember floating around the lazy river at the water amusement park one day when I was off work. I felt sick, but I felt accepted. It was all fun and games, right? Things that teenagers "just do," right?

That summer, I also realized the power that came along with being a friendly, attractive, and sharp 15-year-old teenager. Being late after breaks at work due

32

to flirting with other lifeguards was always taken care of by flashing a smile to my male bosses. I was still watching my water, right?

I dated several guys and led many of them on and enjoyed it. I did not want a boyfriend or anything remotely related to commitment. I liked a challenge. I liked the game. I had never played this one, so I thought it was fun. I never gave these guys even close to what they wanted (although I finally had my first kiss), but I sure knew how to bat my pretty blue eyes and play the game. I used my looks, personality, charm, and intelligence to my advantage, but not always in the best way. It seemed pride was immediately getting to my head once I realized I was attractive and *no longer too shy* to flirt. I thought I had discovered the key to it all. Perhaps what I discovered also played a role in opening the door to my fall later in life—pride.

I carried some of these new behaviors into my junior year of high school. When I returned to school after summer break, people at school started to notice a change in me. Yes, I had started dressing a bit trendier rather than my own preppy and classic style, but this *change* was more than simply "changing my clothes."

At the beginning of the year, I remember a popular boy in my class saying, "Something is different about you. You used to be so innocent." I do not think he was referring to my trendier style of dress. Perhaps the change was evident in my eyes.

I remember thinking, "I'm tired of being innocent 'goody-goody' Lyndsay! I'm tired of being the 'good' girl! I'm tired of being viewed as perfect!"

However, the real change was within my heart. My light was not as bright as it had been because I was slowly drawing further away from God. I was beginning to forget my identity in Christ as I wandered from Him, and I was getting deceived by the enemy, who was telling me righteousness was boring. I pulled away from my best friend, and church became less of a priority. I started becoming friends with other girls who wanted to have fun on the weekends. This year, I was ready to get more than just *tipsy*; I was ready to get wasted.

I felt I needed a *break*. I needed a *break* from my overachiever mindset! I needed a *break* from my struggle to be the perfect student and daughter! But the problem was, I was often extreme in all I did.

Later in life, that "break" in an "extreme way" almost broke me. Thank goodness God placed the pieces back together in time! It was a very slow break and a perfectly-timed recovery that certainly was not instantaneous—but the process of getting to the point of needing recovery was not instantaneous either. The deception of the enemy was slow and carefully crafted. The enemy looked for any opportunity to step in when I was not following the voice of the Lord or making time for Him.

Homecoming that year was very different than previous years when I had gone with amazing guys who went to my church. They had treated me like a princess and brought me home right after the school dance. This year, I went with a cute popular boy who had a group of friends who were ready to party. Prior to the event, I showed them what I had learned that past summer: how to drink—a lot—very quickly.

After chugging something very strong with a name I had never heard of right before we piled into the stretch Hummer the boys had rented to take us to the dance, a guy who I was told had recently been released from jail and did not go to our high school hit me on the head with the bottle I had been drinking. Because I drank so quickly, I was already blacked-out.

The drinking show apparently had backfired. Instead of going to the Homecoming event at school, we ended up at a toga party with both high school and college students, where I somehow lost my date due to my intoxication.

Thank goodness a senior from high school I did not know recognized me and immediately removed me from the party and brought me to a close girlfriend's house where I was supposed to spend the night after the dance. She was not home yet, but her older brother and his college friends positioned me on the couch in a way that I wouldn't choke on my own vomit. I woke up in the morning on the living room floor with a rag on my head, dizzy and baffled. I did not know where I was at first. My girlfriend came downstairs, as did her older brother. I was told the next day that a group of guys at the party were trying to take advantage of me in a private bedroom immediately before I was rescued from the situation. Thank goodness for God's grace and perfect timing. I am also very grateful for this girlfriend, her friend who rescued me from the party, and her kind brother.

I remember feeling guilt and embarrassment, but I had yet to learn my lesson. Weeks later, when the newness of this event faded, I began participating in drinking again. I was determined to be more careful. This time, I only drank with close girlfriends whom I trusted.

When I drank on a Saturday night, it also meant telling my parents I was not going to church Sunday morning, especially if we hit the clubs in Atlanta. Being almost a year younger than my girlfriends in my grade meant a fake 18-year-old ID at age 17 that would get me into the 18 and up clubs. Although drinking and driving was the norm, we never faced any legal consequences. I typically was nervous about anyone driving intoxicated before the night began, but that fear faded once I was intoxicated. Being the youngest and subsequently the last person to get my license kept me from being the driver. Regardless, I often rode with others who drove intoxicated.

Although we never got in any car wrecks, there were costs of my reckless behavior emotionally. Drinking opened the door to various unhealthy patterns. Letting loose on the weekends with alcohol had become my escape that I thought allowed me to truly be me. I saw it as just fun, not realizing I literally was stopping myself from growth emotionally and putting myself in potentially dangerous situations.

Not being in the church on a regular basis also hindered my spiritual growth. I began to learn to lead a double-life. On the outside, life appeared normal and prosperous. I excelled in school and in many other activities that came with recognition. I appeared to be a leader, but I was not always an example on the weekends.

I appeared to be a "perfect" student and example at school, but I also was very good at suppressing my guilt and shame of doing what I knew I was wrong. I
36

was not living a Christian lifestyle, but I was good at putting on a mask and pretending that everything was perfect. I began to feel less emotion over time. If I did feel it, I ran from it.

I remember the night I was crowned pageant queen my junior year of high school. During the final round of selection, I was asked, "What do you consider to be your strongest trait?" My answer was *determination*, but today, I would say, "My ability to allow the Lord to move in my life. My faith."

———————————————

It is *faith* that moves mountains, and it's a freely given gift as a believer in Christ. Determination is a valuable trait, but I know that I cannot accomplish my ultimate purpose without the Holy Spirit! Thank goodness that God's grace is sufficient for us. Grace is His power in our weaknesses.

Today, I can boast in my weaknesses. I do not have to wear a mask. Wearing masks to appear flawless is never fun, because it is based on a false sense of security. It is also draining. True security is in Christ alone. Regardless of any obstacles in our path, the Lord can give us new strength when we put all our trust in Him. He can assist us with perseverance no matter how challenging the task! We must have faith that He will fulfill His promises.

———————————————

Although I was and still am a very determined individual, I was beginning to carry more and more baggage from unconfessed sins into my life during my third year of high school. I continued with the charade and kept the party going. I allowed myself to get close with some friends that did not have my best interest in mind. Little by little, although I maintained a fabulous front, the baggage of the past was hindering me, and I was ignoring the truth.

I ignored the truth when I decided it would be a great idea to go to the prom with someone my parents were not fond of for good reason. That night turned into a disaster for me as well as my friends. However, it was also a blessing in disguise.

We had purchased everything we would need for partying after prom, including the suite at a very nice hotel in Atlanta. My girlfriends and I had adopted the tactic of telling our parents we would be at one another's house, but the truth always comes out in time. That night, we were caught red-handed.

The evening festivities started out by gathering with our parents at my house, where we ended up waiting for *my* date's entrance. When he finally arrived, sunglasses covered his bloodshot eyes. I noticed, and so did my father. My father immediately sensed the night was *not* headed in the right direction.

Every picture we took at my house before we left in the limo showed not only my disappointment in my date's belated arrival, but also in my disappointment in myself for deciding to go to prom with him.

I smile now when I look at the group picture with my face in my hands as I wanted the night to be over before it even began, but at the time, I was not smiling. Little did I know, my father, who has always been a protector, had a conversation with the limo driver before we left. The limo driver knew who to call if he noticed an ulterior plan up anyone's sleeve.

But we all had more than *something* up our sleeves; we had a well-designed game plan—or at least we thought our scheme was seamless.

Once we left in our limo, everyone began smoking marijuana. This was not something I participated in, although I did plan on drinking after I fulfilled my duties as Vice President of our class at prom. However, I became high off contact as the windows of the limo were closed. When we arrived at prom, I was embarrassed and angry that I had put myself in that position. I ducked and hid from others as much as possible as I waited for the effects of the drug to pass. I was completely stressed. After we left, I knew I could finally relax and start drinking at our hotel.

However, God had other plans. Upon walking outside of the prom venue, I saw my father in the distance standing with others by our limo. I felt like a little girl. *Why did he have to ruin this night of all nights?*

My father and the other parents who had come along stood there, arms folded, and watched as we hesitantly approached the limo. They had discovered enough of our carefully constructed after-prom blueprint to step in and save us.

I remember my date snapping at my father; my dad later told me he was furious and had to refrain from responding in the flesh. My father allowed me to ride with the others as they were dropped off one-by-one, but I was ordered to then come home immediately. The individual within our group who held the money for the suite never returned any of it to us. It was not a fun evening. That night, I heard the phrase I had heard in my last year of middle school after being caught smoking, "Lyndsay, you are grounded."

However, what felt like a disaster was a blessing in disguise—which is why I smile today. What seemed like a disappointment at the time was a demonstration of love from both the loving God that I serve and the loving parents He gave me. I was planning on losing my virginity that night, and God protected me from losing that to someone who clearly did not value me, nor show respect towards my parents. Who knows what could have happened that night, especially with the way the night had started.

This night served as a major warning of what could happen if I continued making the wrong choices instead of the right ones—associating with negative influences—drinking—and more importantly, putting God on the backburner and ignoring His guidance.

God sends us warnings along our journey in life, much like the warning signs we see when we are approaching a construction zone. Some state: "Work zone. Speeding fees doubled." This is for our own protection. They are for purpose. When God is working on us and we ignore Him, we miss the lesson He knows we need for the next step chapter of our lives. The next time we fail to listen, the consequences are often harsher.

Fueled by my own will, I ignored this lesson from prom night along with all the roadwork signs. I thought the easy way out would allow me to bypass this route, but I took another detour that only brought me back to repeating the course.

God tried to slow me down to prevent me from of continuing along this detour, but despite being "grounded," I wanted to keep pushing the limits. When my parents refused to allow me to go to the beach with my friends without parental supervision during Spring Break, I found my own fun even when forced to go to a nearby beach with my parents and younger sister. I was certainly becoming very rebellious, but I considered it to be okay, as I had great grades and a good reputation.

After Spring Break, my Junior year was wrapping up, and I got a summer job working as a lifeguard and swim instructor at an outdoor camp on the lake. It was one of the greatest summers of my life, and I spent most of my time with high school girlfriends who worked as camp counselors as well as other employees. After work, we often went wakeboarding and water skiing, activities I loved. My parents often allowed me to take their boat out with my friends alone.

Although those I became close with that summer were not angels, I have very fond memories of the times we all spent together. However, I do not have fond memories of some of the events that took place when I associated with other groups of friends that summer.

One night, a friend from school suggested we sneak out of my parent's basement as I had done on a few occasions, although I had never gone too far from the house nor done anything risky. I had to work very early the next morning, but I agreed to leave and drive with my friend to another friend's house under the condition it would be a quick visit. I did not feel comfortable about the entire situation and refused to drink much—if anything—as I had to be up and alert early the next morning.

Sneaking out of the house led to walking straight into a bad situation. I fell into temptation based on influences from peers that suggested I follow the crowd. Again, I was attempting to gain approval from others—in this case, a girlfriend who had told me I was the last virgin at school and that this was a negative thing. I listened to her words rather than God's, and I suffered the emotional consequences later, as the situation left me overwhelmed with guilt, shame, and remorse. Again, disobeying my parents was not the correct choice.

This choice was one that haunted me for years. I lost my virginity that night to a former boyfriend. I was afraid to say "no" because I wanted to be accepted by others. I still cared for him, although I knew he was not emotionally available. I was a willing volunteer in this situation simply because I wanted to be accepted.

Unfortunately, being a volunteer in that situation led to being a victim in another at that same location while I was asleep after drinking heavily only two or three weeks later. I should not have been there in the first place, as I had lied to my parents again about where I was spending the night. The mother of the person who lived here was very lackadaisical as far as what went on in the house as compared to other parents, so it was the place we all spent the night and partied, although we were told to not drink and drive.

That night, reckless behavior of another form *did* occur. I was raped by a friend of the former boyfriend whom I had lost my virginity to only weeks before this night. However, this time, I *did* say said "no." Repeatedly. Unfortunately, the student who raped me did not listen.

I was filled with shame and confusion immediately after it happened. It certainly sobered me up enough to walk down the stairs to where my girlfriends were. I did not have an opportunity to express what happened to anyone, as he immediately made it clear that we had "slept" together. He was praised by his buddies, which confused me even more. I said nothing.

I felt that because I had not said "no" to my former boyfriend who was friends with this student, I somehow deserved this. I considered it my fault.

I began to hide my shame and pain deep inside my heart, put on a more disguising mask, and simply not feel my feelings. My self-worth depleted, and many of my mindsets began to change. I thought what happened was just normal—something guys just do.

I learned to numb myself and continued to cover up my shame, disgust, and fear with alcohol because it blocked my emotions. At first, drinking had just been for "fun," but now, I began to drink to not have to think—think about the shame—the guilt.

In my distorted perception, I still saw drinking as a fun, normal activity—a way to pretend everything was okay. I did not see it as a destructive coping tool, which it clearly had become after that experience took place.

At times, this coping mechanism placed me in additional compromising situations. I developed problems with setting boundaries with others and saying "no" in various situations. If I ever felt used or ashamed, I ignored the pain, I did not let anyone know anything was wrong, and I attempted to forget anything bad ever happened.

Deep inside, I blamed myself. I was deceived. I had also forgotten about God's forgiveness. Instead, my burden of shame became heavy. I did not let go of the baggage I was carrying by laying it at the cross, nor did I remember there is no condemnation in Christ. Instead, I saw myself as dirty—as a whore. I assumed everyone who knew about this saw this when they looked at me.

Although I could not forgive myself, a new boyfriend who never pressured me in any way literally stepped into my life at the perfect time. We had a healthy friendship and relationship. He attempted to shelter me from participating in the heavy drugs I had started to notice at parties. He was very much a protector in general and a wonderful person. I believe he saw my naivety and curiosity, knew the damage it could cause, and responded by sheltering me from it as much as possible, despite my pleas to "just try it." But I fell into temptation after the relationship ended for unrelated reasons. *(Side note: I will note that this former boyfriend and I remained close friends for many years well into my twenties, and I will always be thankful for him!)*

At the age of 16, ecstasy was a major drug available in the area for high school kids, and raves—organized underground dance parties filled with people selling and/or on ecstasy—were the new rave. I loved "rave" music, and I loved the feeling associated with ecstasy. I did not see the harm in the drug, as I felt it was a time for my girlfriends and I to bond. We did this on occasion, as well as during Spring Break my senior year, when we went without direct parental supervision. This time, I had been allowed to go, as my parents and sister would be at a nearby beach in Florida.

44

However, I tended to go much further than my girlfriends that Spring Break. After taking ecstasy and enjoying "deep" conversations with my close girlfriends, I wandered off into the darkness, looking for whatever would continue to feed my high. In the process, I remember seeing my sister, now a high school freshman, who looked beyond bewildered by the way I was acting.

Later that night, my friends became concerned when I was gone for some time, as I had found another drug to try that night. At some point, the male friends we went with rescued me from my demise by removing me from the situation.

The remainder of my senior year of high school, I was more serene and composed in all aspects of my life, perhaps because I was often grounded! *Thank God for that!* I sang "The Wind Beneath My Wings" at our baccalaureate service with an intelligent and strong Christian girl who was in many of my Advanced Placement and honors classes who boldly proclaimed God's truth no matter who was listening or watching. I looked up to her and her confidence in who she was in Christ, completely unashamed of her faith. She always had a Bible on her desk. Although she never judged me, I knew she was aware I was walking a thin line, as God-fearing women have discernment and are shown the truth. You cannot hide the truth from those who know God's truth!

The song we sang was appropriate, because I knew that the Lord had certainly carried me through those years. I was accepted into a top-notch university, along with the close girlfriend whom I had met my freshman year. Most of the girls I was closest with went to other colleges, but we promised to not let the distance impact our friendships.

I graduated from my high school with numerous awards, and judging by our class graduation picture, I had more tassels from various honors societies than anyone else in my class. I certainly had worked very hard for those awards, but I was still wearing a mask that hid the truth; my other side. A dark side. I was walking a double-line.

---

*When the waves begin to crash around us after wandering off course, it is a beautiful thing to be **carried** above those waves by the one who **carried** the cross. No moment is too late to change course and fix our eyes on the Lord, our anchor that stabilizes us along the waves of life. He is our refuge, our fortress, and our safe harbor during every storm. When we trust in Him, no wave can **break** us. What a beautiful thing to know Christ is there, holding us...loving us. In Him, we are safe. His love for us is **unbreakable**.*

Chapter Four: Safe Harbor

*Have mercy on me, my God, have mercy on me, for in you
I take refuge. I will take refuge in the shadow of your
wings until the disaster has passed."
~Psalms 57:1*

So off to college I went at the age of 17. I had the
opportunity to make my own decisions and take what
I acquired in my primary and secondary education and
apply it to life. I chose to align myself with individuals
who were also determined to be successful.

One of my first decisions independent of my parents
was which sorority to join. Rush was a major event at
my university, and thousands of students went
through the process. Once one joined a sorority, she
was immediately placed somewhere along the social
status hierarchy within the Greek system; thus, for
many, it was a high-pressure situation. Although I
personally saw it as exciting and enjoyable rather than
a source of stress, I considered it necessary to be
affiliated with intelligent, classy, outgoing, well-
rounded women, and I did indeed become a member
of a sorority that was unquestionably viewed as
exceptional.

My new group of sisters were beautiful, confident
women who maintained high academic standing and
had a wonderful reputation within the community. In
fact, they seemed almost…well, perfect. It was highly
desirable to be a part of this group. They certainly
knew how to present themselves well, as did I. I fit
right in and was so excited to be a part of this group.
Apparently, I had chosen wisely when making my
selection to rate them as my first choice, and I was
blessed that they too had chosen me to be a part of

their new pledge class. I loved my new sisters, who took us under their wings, showered us with gifts, and were beyond supportive. My big sis was amazing, and I loved the positive energy I felt when I was around my sisters and in the sorority house.

The women in our sorority had high standards for behavior, which is what I had longed for in high school, although I did not exactly see a plethora of exemplary role models during my high school years. Yes, there were plenty of amazing well-behaved students, but I do not remember often thinking, "I want to be like her." I longed to find classy, sophisticated, confident women who also maintained excellent grades, were involved on campus, and could still have fun and be social without pushing the limits. This was exactly what the Lord gave me in joining this sorority. Many of these women were great examples for me as a new college student.

Thus, I tried to erase any negative memories from the later years of high school by being well-behaved, which for me meant continuing to stay very focused on school and positive activities along with being social yet conservative. I typically limited my drinking during my freshman year, as I cared very much about my reputation and how I presented myself to others. I wanted to be in control and stay focused on school, yet still have a healthy social life.

I was successful at this. I received excellent grades and had perfect attendance to all the weekly meetings, various functions, and social events within my sorority. I became a "little sister" of a fraternity and involved with various events on campus.

Indeed, college life was wonderful. I lived in a small dorm room that barely held a third of my clothes, but fortunately, I roomed with a close friend from high school, and we got along well. Although we were in different social groups, we laughed and were carefree when together in our tiny room, often finding ourselves reminiscing about high school memories. I don't think she meant it for ridicule or hurt in any way, but as we recalled our high school days, some of the events that arose in conversation evoked feelings of shame when names of certain individuals arose. I obviously never told my roommate the truth about what happened the night when I was taking advantage of the summer before my senior year.

Meanwhile, the enemy was at work early on to make me feel condemned by past hurts when those painful high school memories became lost in translation. I know my roommate meant no harm, but certain words traveled from her, to some of her fraternity friends, to board members of my sorority. Apparently, rumor had it that certain sexual escapades were taking place in our dorm room that resulted in nicknames. This was most definitely a rumor. Honestly, thinking about it reminds me of the telephone game.

When I was called in to speak to a few of my sisters, very little information was given as to why I was there. In fact, I walked away wondering why I had been asked to speak with them about my behavior. It tore me apart wondering what I had done that was wrong in their eyes. I had certainly been reliable, classy, and punctual. I maintained great grades and had perfect attendance at all events. I had also stepped up to leadership positions within our sorority. I was baffled.

I thought back to what I could have possible done that may have appeared trashy or unsophisticated at any

49

point in time, and I could not think of anything. I remained confused and clueless as to why I was petitioned to speak to them until the last week of my freshman year, when a pledge sister I trusted nonchalantly mentioned it in passing. Apparently, someone had told her. She was so loving and kind about it, but my jaw dropped. She had no idea that I was never given an explanation, and she had no idea how this information triggered the trauma from my past.

I was shocked, hurt, and felt even more condemnation when these lies of the enemy led to me being gently scolded by my sorority for something which never took place. These ladies were not harsh whatsoever in how they spoke with me, and I feel it was appropriate to have a conversation. I had placed the painful memory of what I had experienced behind me when I entered college. It was simply the enemy working behind the scenes, causing miscommunication and trying to rub my past in my face to make me feel shame. It worked. However, I had yet to process what had happened when I was raped.

This incident of being taken advantage of resurfaced in my mind along with certain decisions that followed, including the self-destructive attempts to cover those memories. Thus, my self-esteem suffered once again, although this was still not apparent on the outside by any means. I was chosen by my sorority to be a greeter for fall rush, which meant I would be one of the two faces first seen by thousands of rushees. I would be their first impression before opening the doors to lead them to where the rest of the girls were waiting to start enthusiastic "walk songs" which spoke of our joy of being a part of such an amazing group of women.

Perhaps I was very good at putting on a mask and always appearing "perfect," despite how I felt on the inside. Perhaps I was almost too good at this. In fact, perhaps I was getting better and better at wearing a mask to hide my feelings. Or, maybe I *was* a good example within the group of women. Either way, I had an amazing time serving in this role, and I was excited to represent my sisters in this way.

As the first year of college concluded, I moved back to my hometown for the summer, starting it off by accepting a supply teaching position in the county teaching French to middle school students during the month of May. I lifeguarded once again at the same location with a close high school girlfriend, waited tables, and spent time with my other close high school girlfriends. We had a great summer, and as it concluded, my excitement for my upcoming sophomore year of college grew.

This year, I lived in our sorority house, which was set up as a courtyard between the main house and a row of adjacent yet separate two and four-bedroom apartments. I moved into a four-bedroom apartment with two of my closest friends. I had found out earlier in the summer while visiting my best friend who would have been our fourth roommate that she was transferring to another university, which was very disappointing, but I had a blast with my other close sisters.

The year was off to a great start. Being on the other side of rush was a wonderful experience. We had a new group of stunning pledges, and I became a big sis to an amazing new little sis. I chose to major in psychology rather than pre-law, which had my original plan. My classes were going wonderful. A new football season began, and I joined my sororities' chorale as well as the University's Glee Club with one of my roommates, who also loved to sing.

Although my sorority sisters seemed perfect, I later learned that like everyone, they too were not without flaws. I noticed several of them had deep wounds that led to eating disorders and self-mutilation, which I did not understand. I remember thinking how blessed I was for not feeling the need to harm myself with those self-destructive behaviors. I accredited it to growing up in a wonderful family and being disciplined.

Little did I know, I *did* have a self-destructive behavioral pattern that was slowly causing destruction, even if little by little. Fall semester, a friend became very hurt by a decision I made, although this was not my intention. Of course, drinking was involved. This was the first instance in which alcohol affected a relationship with someone I deeply treasured. Losing the closeness of our friendship was very hard on me and was another consequence of ignoring the Lord's guidance to avoid drinking. God was no longer on my list of top priorities.

On the outside, I held it together very well, but deep on the inside, my heart was filled with guilt, shame, and regret, not only because of this situation, but other situations involving drinking and men. I then began picking up the self-destructive habits of others simply due to proximity. I continued to be easily influenced.

I remembered seeing a friend who always seemed to smiling cut her wrist with a razor, although she never knew I saw her doing this. I wondered if that might help my pain as it seemed to help her keep on her smile, so I took the razor I used to shave my legs and barely nicked the side of my wrist one night while intoxicated and filled with regret. Although there was no blood, I felt a rush. If only I would have given my burden to God and allowed myself to feel the rush of His freely-given grace washing over me. But I ran from it, and I ran towards what others were doing to escape their own pain.

In fact, due to my guilt from what had happened between my close friend and me, I ran from the situation and moved to the other side of the sorority house in a new apartment with some of my other pledge sisters. These sisters were also amazing, and God continued to give me open doors in new areas and friendships. However, the enemy began placing traps and new temptations around me through new associations.

I was still very naïve, trusting, and easily manipulated by others at this age. I gravitated towards some people who did not necessarily make the best decisions while drinking. I had yet to grasp the importance of choosing my friends carefully and was easily led off a righteous path after my school work was done. Regardless, my grades were top notch, I was focused on leading a large event as the new Philanthropy Chair in my sorority, and I refrained from allowing going out or drinking to affect my studies or my work-out routines. I placed strong limits on when I ventured out with friends, because I knew when I did, it would mean recovery time. Being very studious and diligent, I continued to refuse to place my social life before my studies, workouts, or other responsibilities, regardless of what others decided to do. But I did not leave any time for God.

Time spent with one individual typically led to trouble. I had ignored past warning signs to keep my distance from her, but we had a great time together, although we seemed to feed off one another once we started drinking. I believe we both received a warning from the Lord after a minor car accident, but instead of heeding His protection, we laughed it off and continued to head towards our destination. We resorted to forgetting about it by downing liquor. I should have taken that night as a warning that perhaps I should revaluate my choices. Instead, I did not heed His counsel, and eventually, I got burned.

I chose to live with several of my sisters in a nice apartment outside of campus my junior year. We were very excited to have a first apartment, and we were thrilled to be living in "the place to be" as students at our university, especially due to the pool being "party central" during spring and summer and the community being very active in terms of resident social events. A nice bonus was the job I got at the complex leasing apartments and serving as the "community assistant" of my building.

I loved this job as well as my new residence. It allowed me to live for free and get compensated for sales. My parents had agreed to pay for my apartment, as they had provided for me 100% during college, and they wanted me to learn to make the most out of the money I was making. Thus, they provided me with the funds that they would have paid for my apartment.

Early that year, I met a new male transfer who quickly became my boyfriend. We became inseparable from the start, but my studies always remained my top priority. I considered him my first true love at that point. Prior to this, I never saw the value of being with one person long-term, nor had I ever wanted to commit to a real relationship due to past hurts. I only had eyes for him, I was very loyal, and I allowed myself to be vulnerable with my feelings for the first time. I began to desire something lasting.

However, our weekend lifestyle caused a strain on our relationship. I began to pull away from sorority events as he was not in a fraternity. I spent less time with my girlfriends, as he took their place. I often was a wreck when drinking, so it was very important for me to show my "loyalty" to my boyfriend by spending all my time with him when not working or studying. I certainly allowed him to influence my choices, such as which friends were good influences. Regardless of his true motives, I perceived his suggestions as controlling. I see now that he did indeed see the change in me when I was around certain people who were more of "drinking buddies" than true friends. Bottom line, he saw the change in me when I decided to drink, which was no one's choice but my own.

However, one night when I was studying for a test the next morning, my boyfriend went out with several friends, including a close girlfriend of mine. I will spare the details, but I will say I discovered something the next morning that broke my heart that involved him and this close girlfriend.

After this discovery, I rushed to take my test in tears after being told he had been loyal to me. I am not sure if I believed him or not, but I knew I did not want to lose him. I allowed him back in my life, and he even moved into my complex in the building across from mine. From that point forward, we were together almost every minute aside from working and attending our classes. We practically lived together.

However, the relationship came to a halt at the end of my junior year. Soon after, I learned that him and the "close friend" mentioned above were now dating.

Obviously, this made me question a lot that had happened earlier in the year. It broke my heart.

As a community assistant of my building and having signed a lease for the next year, I was going to have to tough it out with living more than just *close* to them, regardless of the circumstances. Perhaps God was attempting to bring me closer to my first true love, Jesus.

I had let my former boyfriend lead me in choosing my friends and how much time I spend with them, so I had grown apart from many of my girlfriends and felt very alone during that time. One of the friends he told me to stay away from was now his new girlfriend. I was so confused and heartbroken. However, I will tell you that this was many years ago, and time has healed all pain. I have no ill will for either party; I am simply sharing this experience to express how it changed my personal decisions and actions down the line as I did not fully deal with the grief I experienced during this time.

Fortunately, I had become close with another girl a bit younger than me, and we spent a lot of time at her apartment, which was also in the complex. She started working at the leasing office as well.

I cried to her often. I was depressed every time I heard my former boyfriend's loud truck enter the complex, as my apartment was right near the entrance. My heart was broken, and I certainly had a front row seat to view my him and his new girlfriend together.

I became depressed and went into therapy at the university. I began having panic attacks and severe stomach aches. I ran miles every morning, and I rarely wanted to eat. I am toned yet also thin, but during this time, I was certainly underweight. I simply had no appetite.

I positively coped by learning guitar and singing to the songs I played, spending time with my new best friend, and studying for the GRE, as I would be applying for graduate school in psychology in several months.

Then something amazing happened. In my pain, I drew closer to God. I picked up my journal and decided that I would let it all out to Him. One journal entry in September of 2002 reads, "nothing makes me happy anymore." As you will soon see, that decision to journal became something that I still do today; a decision that inspired the writing of this book.

My journal entries today are much different, but during this time of my life, they were filled with great sorrow and desperation. Yet the Lord used it all; nothing is ever wasted. You are reading much of the summarized version of my journal entries now, and I hope that you can use it for gain. If my own life lessons are of some value to you, then I know every bit of pain I experienced was well worth it. Pain does have a purpose. It certainly made me stronger.

While I was not in a place of understanding this wisdom at the age of 20, there would be a time for this revelation down the road. Although I was beginning to learn some valuable coping skills amid new trials, my panic attacks persisted, and I became deeply depressed. I started isolating and acting out, finding myself "attracted to scandalous situations and losers," as noted in my journal. After drinking, I would wake up feeling depressed, which I described as "that horrible feeling of guilt I have in my stomach." I even went as far as to write, "I have a serious drinking problem, and I need AA." I was aware that "I struggled with substance abuse and sexuality."

It was a blessing that I could admit these struggles to the Lord through writing, but I had yet to learn to completely surrender these areas to Christ and let His grace wash away the guilt, shame, and pain. Instead of keeping my eyes fixed on the Lord and steering clear of the stumbling blocks that had only led to hurt in the past, I continued to act out in ways that ended up hurting others and ultimately, myself.

For example, I was filled with pain the night I saw my former boyfriend embrace the woman he was dating at one of our usual bar spots. Looking back now, I should have taken the proper turn and avoided bars all together, regardless that it was "what you do" in college. But once I started drinking, I put myself in a vulnerable position and typically was more depressed.

After I saw them embrace, I darted to the restroom and ran into a friend of his. This person offered me something that would end up being my quick-fix when depressed after consuming alcohol off and on for the next ten years: a substance that was not a depressant, but a stimulant. However, this did not fix anything; it made more of a mess in my life.

A few days later, I journaled about how my introduction to cocaine numbed the pain: "I tried coke this weekend. I was upset, drunk, and it did make me feel better. I got upset on Saturday, and I took some more. I was so depressed all day, and I just wanted someone to lay with me and tell me everything is okay. I just want to fall in love again, but I am afraid I never will." However, God loved me more than ever, and He was holding me tightly.

Despite my darkest thoughts, I still had enough faith and gratitude to write: "This time of my life has brought me closer to you, God." This little mustard seed of faith was all I needed to get through this moment in time. God was at work even then. He always completes what He begins. He knew what He was doing, and He heard my prayers and praises.

I did get through it, of course. I also learned many valuable lessons. This lesson taught me that when I lose something, such as a relationship, it is for a reason. In most cases, I must let it go and trust that God has something much better in store for me, as He knows His daughter best.

———————⟨⟨ ℞ ⟩⟩———————

Instead of trying to find other things to fill a void from something that didn't quite fit in the first place, we must forgive ourselves, surrender to the Lord's process, and move on, open to the precious things that await us along the journey of life.

If there are things in our lives that do not come from God that block our vision, how can we see the gifts along the shoreline, just waiting for God to shine His light down from above so that we can receive His freely-given treasures? If there are things in our hands that do not come from Him, how can we raise our arms to accept what He wants to pour down from the Heavens?

———————⟨⟨ ℞ ⟩⟩———————

By the grace of God, I surrendered the relationship and picked up my journal, guitar, and graduate school submission packets. I made the decision to stay focused and wait on God's treasures for the remainder of my senior year. I was also certain that my acceptance into various programs would put me in higher spirits, as my achievements always seemed to do. In my mind, it would solve all my problems. In terms of accomplishments, I had yet to truly experience an instance in which I was not successful in my goal. I had yet to learn how to handle defeat.

But God wanted to stretch my faith. It was time. Regardless of my high grades, strong Statement of Purpose, various internships, positions within the psychology department, and jobs conducting various research on top of my leasing position, I did *not* make it into any of the top-notch programs to which I applied. Apparently, God had a reason for that as well. It was simply not time!

This was a major hit to my pride. I don't think I had ever faced rejection when it came to academics or involvements with extra-curricular activities even remotely close to this extent. However, God had something better down the line, and I would eventually see this. Often, what seems to be "rejection" is God's protection!

I continued to face bouts of anxiety, panic attacks, and depression. On my 21st birthday, although I was determined to only drink one glass of wine, I was sick in the bar restroom by midnight, and I was in my bed soon after that. I could not control my drinking, no matter what I tried. I wanted to, but I simply could not.

When I awoke from my haze that Halloween morning, I wrote this passage in my journal to God: "Thinking of drugs and sex disgusts me. I want you to lead me

60

down the right path. Take away my worries, stress, and confusion. Be my Protector and Savior and Comforter. Lead me to a Christian life. Mold my life and help me through everything. Thank you for healing me. I promise to stop drinking. I promise."

I longed for the comfort of Jesus, but at the time, I was not letting go of the things that had held me back from worries, stress, and confusion. I didn't stop with the drugs, and after any level of physical intimacy, I only was left feeling dirty. God still heard my prayers. In fact, He had already answered them in Heaven's time.

During this dark season of my life, the Lord used my new best friend to comfort and encourage me. Our times together are some of my fondest memories. However, some of our adventures, or rather my decisions during our adventures, did not result in comfort in the long run.

We decided to leave our college town every so often on the weekends to get away. We found ourselves in the club scene of Atlanta, where her new boyfriend hosted events at various venues. Here, we "worked" the VIP rooms and met "celebrities," yet we were basically paid to have fun, drink for free, socialize, and ultimately serve as eye candy. It was anything but glorious when I think about it today, although I enjoyed being in the "spotlight" in those dark places.

Today, I hope that my light shines wherever God places me for His glory. I am by no means perfect, but only God could orchestrate this amazing change in my life; a complete divine reversal on the enemy.

Looking back at those last few months of college, I was still searching for something—anything—to feel complete on the inside after a broken relationship that left me vulnerable and wounded. I was deceived by discovering counter-productive distractions which kept me occupied. These quick "feel-good" pick-me-ups which focused on outward appearances lied to me, telling me that I did not have to deal with my pain. I could simply fake it. I faked it so well that those empty sources of fulfillment turned into patterns that created mindsets that were not centered on the Word but on the world. I was forgetting my identity in Christ and becoming further out of alignment with His plan for my life.

One of these mindsets? Entitlement. I realized I could use my looks and charm to pass the long lines to the clubs and walk right in, a mindset that would continue well into my twenties until I realized I did not want to be a part of the party lifestyle.

Spending time in this environment also exposed me to more darkness, including drugs, deceit, corruption, evil, and potentially life-threatening situations that were a parents' nightmare. However, I still was naïve and believed that no one had an impure motive to harm *me*. Criminals? In my mind, they were somewhere else. Anywhere but all around me, regardless of what my mother had told me numerous times as I was walking out the door.

Not only did I step into this dark world, but I pulled my younger sister smack dab in the middle of this fruitless scene one evening. When I was ready for the night to end, we both walked ahead to my new car, where we sat waiting for my closest friend, her boyfriend, and another friend who was our designated driver. I was ready to leave and began calling them repeatedly from the parking lot across from the venue.

Today, I know that it is my responsibility to lead my younger sister by example, but I was not exactly a role model that evening. God placed me in a position of leadership as her older sister, and I was not being obedient to His order as her big sis. I was intoxicated, but my younger sister held her composure.

Suddenly, a man approached us from the passenger side of the vehicle where my sister was seated and demanded our purses and cell phones. He placed a gun to my sister's leg, but I was unaware of this at the time. My answer to his question? "No!" My sister's response? What my mother had always instructed us to say if ever in danger: "I rebuke you in the name of Jesus Christ."

There *is* power in the name of Jesus. And He certainly demonstrated His power that night through His protection.

The man managed to snatch the only purse He could grab—mine—and then, I made another horrible decision: I kicked off my stilettos and pursued the mugger into an alley in attempts to rescue my purse, which I did. In fact, *he* was the one running from *me*.

Although I was not acting wisely, the enemy runs when rebuked in the most power name of all: Jesus. I am so thankful the Holy Spirit prompted my sister to remember and use those words. I am so thankful for the protection of my loving Heavenly Father despite my foolishness. The key to all is held in the name of Jesus.

Yet in my invincible state of mind, I proudly boasted about how *I* retrieved the purse when I strutted back to the vehicle. I laughed it off, although my sister remembers being worried I might never return while I was gone for what seemed like less than a minute to me, but hours to her.

Instead of praising God for *His* protection and saving grace, *I* wanted to be praised. I ushered my sister back into the club to find my friends, where I accepted the shots of "sympathy" from the owners of the nightclub. Here, I continued to boast of my strength to the others, but the true power was God's strength in my weakness. His powerful grace. Yes, the true power was and is and is forevermore in the name of Jesus. He is my safe harbor.

At that time, I was floating astray, drifting further and further from what was safe. I would learn later that there would be consequences for my disobedience and pride, and it would come with the beautiful gift of humility, which was indeed a blessing in disguise for a season.

But humility was not my strong suit during this season. Are you curious to know the brutally honest reason why I ran after the man who attempted to steal my purse? Entitlement and selfishness. When my father sat me down over dinner to ask why, I had no problem telling him that not having my purse meant not having an ID the next night, which meant not being able to walk right back into the world of the "creatures of the night," as my best girlfriend and I called them. I failed to listen to that guidance yet again. I ignored my father and my Heavenly Father.

Yes, I was selfish and a complete fool, but God did not allow any serious harm to come my way. He had other plans to turn my ashes into beauty, my battle scars into art, and my pain into purpose.

Although I was becoming what I looked down at with disgust and judgement, a "creature of the night," I thought that being accomplished disqualified me from this description. My grades, achievements, and ability to hold myself together on the "outside" served as my justification that partying it up on the weekends was perfectly fine. I thought I was comfortable with this, but the Lord saw the inner battle within my heart, even though I did not want to stop to listen long enough to hear my own heartbeat.

Regardless, it was not God's time for major consequences yet, and I graduated from college with a double major in Psychology and Sociology, an almost perfect GPA, and a list of achievements to go along with the long list of areas that God had plans to refine. Thank goodness He knew just what He was doing.

Eventually, God allowed me to be placed in a position when I finally decided I was finished with repetitive lessons that got tougher and tougher and gradually caused undeniable pain until I was ready to hold up my white flag of surrender and listen to His guidance. I once saw that position as painful and frustrating, but I later realized that here, He was cradling me; He was placing me back in His safe harbor, protected under the shelter of His wings. He allowed this only because of His love for me. He simply wanted me to listen.

When we fail to heed His gentle guidance, The Lord will allow us to walk through the same lesson over and over until we listen. He will knock louder and louder on the doors of our heart until we surrender to His plan. He only allows the consequences He knows we can handle when and if it is needed. *Why?* He knows what is best for His children, He knows our destiny and what we need to accomplish His plans, and He knows the greatness He has prepared for us in His perfect time.

I am blessed that I was placed directly in His safe harbor and was shown His grace and mercy. I am grateful that I eventually chose to go deeper with Him and surrender my past. In the secret place with Him, I received more than just a taste of the fruit that comes from a deep intimacy with God. Today, His presence is what I crave.

What a beautiful thing it is to dwell in the shelter of the Almighty. The Lord is our refuge and fortress in any storm. He is a safe harbor for ships, rest for the weary traveler, strength for the weak, and the director of the waves of the sea.

Chapter Five: Waves Along the Sandbar

Should you not fear me?" declares the LORD. "Should you
not tremble in my presence? I made the sand a boundary
for the sea, an everlasting barrier it cannot cross. The
waves may roll, but they cannot prevail; they may roar, but
they cannot cross it.
~Jeremiah 5:22

Perhaps I had begun to take the love and protection
of God for granted. Perhaps I did not fear Him. We can
forget what holds true value when we latch on to that
which lacks real meaning and does not come from
God, the source of all good and perfect gifts. Today, I
am a God-fearing woman who has allowed God to be
my anchor. I am fully open to the beautiful blessings
He has in store for me, regardless of the waves that
will come along life's journey.

I see now that God can use the "waves of life"—such
as failure to get in graduate school in this case—to
plant us where He does want us so we do not run
ahead of His plan. We must trust His direction and
timing. There is always a reason for a season, even if
we do not fully understand the reason for many
seasons to come. We must always be still and wait on
His direction. Sometimes, He strategically places us
on a "sandbar," forcing us to wait until the time is right
for us to travel to our next destination, but He always
uses those waiting periods for a purpose.

I found myself in the "waiting room" while anticipating
the opening of the right door in terms of graduate
school, but the wait was a bit longer than I expected.
I did not have a plan B, so I began looking for jobs

somewhat related to what I wanted to do after graduate school. I refused to give up on that plan.

Perhaps I needed a small dose of humility before God would fulfill this dream. Perhaps God was using this opportunity as preparation for a transition. Regardless, He was still at work in my life, steering me in the right direction.

I accepted my first job offer working as a recruiter in Atlanta for a small company. I quickly discovered I *hated* this job, often complaining to others that I was not using all my knowledge and skills and had so much more to offer.

Yes, the waves along this passage of my life were bumpy and uncomfortable, but I toughed it out as best as I could. I felt devalued and underappreciated at my workplace. I saw my work as mundane. I was frustrated to say the least. The company seemed to be a revolving door in terms of turnover, which further fueled my determination to enter graduate school in the field of Industrial/Organizational Psychology. This would teach me the skills needed to motivate and empower employees and teach others the leadership skills needed to increase ROI in a corporate setting.

My motivation at my own workplace was very low, but I grew closer to God during this time. I fixed my eyes on Christ and continued to face each day with hope.

When not at the office, I spent the remainder of my time during the weekdays with my roommate, a close friend from college. We had moved into a nice apartment in Atlanta, and we spent much of our time cooking, decorating, planning dinner parties, and working out early in the morning together. After my workouts, I would head to my office in Downtown Atlanta.

One rainy day, I was running late for work. In a panic to arrive on time, I unknowingly got off the incorrect level of my building after being on the elevator with a group of people. I darted towards what I thought was my office door, completely unaware that I was *not* on the proper floor of the building.

As I approached the door, I lifted my head to see this was not my office. Before me was a large sign that read a company name along with the words, "Corporate Psychology/Management Consultants." I did some research and decided working for this company was my dream job.

Little did I know that this was not merely a coincidence. I was placed in front of that door for a reason. No, there are no coincidences in life; the things that we often see as delays, such as traffic on a rainy day that causes us to be late one morning for work, are often divine appointments used for guidance, protection, and other gifts from God.

If we keep our head up high above the waves, fixing our eyes on Jesus, we remain open to receive the blessings He has in store for us. There is so much He longs to show us even in the seemingly mundane! It is important to keep hopeful that He has blessings in place for us, but if we keep our head down and complain about our current situation, we might just miss those blessings!

The "waves" of life can either knock us down or propel us to a new place. Those waves may be out of our control, but it is the Lord who controls them! God knows exactly what is to come, and He knows His perfect timing for new doors to open. It is up to us to choose to walk through those open doors in *His* timing and receive His blessings without focusing on the distractions of the enemy in the meantime.

Meanwhile, I still struggled with certain distractions. Although I was closer with the Lord, I continued to consistently drink with my girlfriends from college on the weekends. I searched for a potential love interest when out on the town. *(Side note: Experience later taught me that whatever I found in a bar, I later lost. I know some may have met their true love in a bar, but I would personally rather stay away from the lessons of my past!)*

Meeting men through friends and social activities within that seemingly "classy" nightlife scene did not bring me joy. I tended to frequent upscale venues, but that did not mean there was a plethora of upstanding individuals inside the doors.

My journal entries consisted of various encounters with men I briefly dated, as I desperately wanted a healthy and loving relationship *without* any real commitment. This paradox is likely the reason God did not answer this prayer! There was not a proper alignment of my heart and mind in terms of relationships. I was praying for one thing, but I was not ready within my heart! I was searching for something in the *wrong* place, at the *wrong* time, with the *wrong* motives.

It was *not* time to meet Mr. Right. I was still in search of myself and not yet ready, although I *thought* that was what I wanted. I found it interesting when I saw a

70

journal entry that confirmed this lesson I failed to see at the time. Someone had lightheartedly said to me, "Don't even talk to me before you're 26, because girls go through this whole 'find yourself' thing." I smiled when I read this years later, knowing that this person was placed in my path. In my case, he was right! I did not know my identity!

One thing I *did* know was I could not take another minute at my job. After prayer, I decided to resign, resorting to substitute teaching while I completed another round of graduate school applications. In the process, I connected with a wonderful professor who had researched topics of great interest to me. I was accepted to start in a program only a few months later, although I would be coming in with a cohort that was a semester ahead of me and about to graduate. I would graduate with the group that started the following semester.

Considered one of the top ten Master's programs in the field of Industrial/Organizational Psychology, my new graduate school in Tennessee was amazing. I took advantage of the fact that I would have an extra semester within the program to do more than one research project, and my research was accepted into the Society for Industrial and Organizational Psychology's annual conference. The topic related to the ability to fake non-cognitive and personality testing measures used for pre-employment selection. Testing and measurement became an area I loved within my field.

After the research was presented at the conference, I received an internship in Human Resources which turned into a full-time job as a Human Resources Generalist. My boss, the Human Resources Manager, had been a graduate of the program, and she was amazing. I fulfilled my duties and handled larger responsibilities when she left on maternity leave, serving as the Human Resources Manager when she was not in the office. I had a lot on my plate, including a graduate assistantship that paid for my classes and came with a stipend.

As my classes continued, the loan I had taken out for graduate school was quickly paid off. My finances were never a problem, and my savings account was in great shape. I received A's in all my classes.

I also loved the group of students that had entered the program a few months after me. In college, my friends all seemed to fit in the same social category. I loved the diversity of our group in graduate school and grew very close with many of them. I felt free to be my nerdy, studious self for the first time. Many of us are still in touch today, and I can honestly say these were some of my favorite times.

We spent our Wednesday nights studying at one another's apartments taking turns cooking meals. We studied together. We laughed, we cried, and we never failed to incorporate statistic jokes into our conversations. We even took road trips together.

We went out to the local bars here and there, but I remained very focused on school and work. I also didn't think the nightlife scene in Tennessee was anything *close* to what it was in Atlanta. I still had a sense of entitlement and somehow prided myself on being somewhat of a social director in my hometown. I grew bored on the weekends and began to crave the lifestyle I had once known. My girlfriends from college who lived in Atlanta repeatedly urged me to come visit, and I began to feel I was missing out if I didn't. When

I finally drove to Atlanta, I was ready to party. I worked hard during the week, so I deserved it, right?

For a moment, I began to let the partying start to spin out of control. At the request of my parents, I reluctantly accepted my father's invitation to see a certified addiction counselor, who told me I was an alcoholic. I rejected his words and sought to discount them. He suggested a local support group, and I followed through with the request, but when I pulled up to an older, rickety building for the first meeting, I decided that I was too good to go inside. I *did* stop drinking for a month to prove I could do it.

I found ways to exercise my conscience, journaling to God about anything that caused me guilt. I made it my goal to be in the Word as much as possible, but I could not seem to stick to it. I remember it taking almost a year to complete a simple daily devotional workbook. I made the excuse that I could not find a church I liked in Tennessee, so I was not fellowshipping with other believers to help strengthen my walk. I cried out to God, but mostly only when I needed Him.

I did things the same way I always had on my 22nd birthday, when I celebrated both my special day and Halloween. I traveled from Tennessee to Atlanta for the weekend to start the night off at one of my favorite restaurants with a large group of friends. Ironically, I was dressed as an angel that year, but I ended up in a situation that left me feeling overwhelmed.

My college girlfriends came to my rescue the following morning to find me in tears, broken angel wings in hand. This was likely was the first time they had seen me cry sober. I had no recollection of the night before and was scared to death. I continued to cry hysterically to my friends all day, not having a clue of what had happened. They were frustrated and eventually told me I had about ten more minutes until the pouting had to end, but they both consoled and lectured me, urging me to refrain from wandering off intoxicated. I did not realize that I was hurting them until that moment. They were very worried. I love those girls, and I am so thankful they were there for me. I am also thankful for the Heavenly angels I know the Lord had around me that night, sheltering me with their mighty wings.

Today, I do not consider clubs or bars my scene. That does not mean I do not love to have fun with others, but fun for me does certainly does not involve drinking to excess and failing to remember the evening! Although I am naturally social, I am quite content with solitude as well, as I know I am never alone; my intimate one-on-one time with Christ is vital to my being. It brings me a perfect peace, fosters my creativity, and allows me to hear God's voice.

But during this time, I was stuck on a "sandbar" rather than moving forward fully anchored in Christ, despite having been a Christian for almost 20 years. I had become lukewarm. I was no longer growing spiritually, and my life was out of balance. I was being tossed by the waves of the sea, looking to the left, the right, and mostly, behind me, burdened by my past.

Instead of leaving my burdens at the altar, being obedient, receiving God's grace, and allowing myself to be still enough to hear God calling my name, I struggled to do it all alone, as I always thought I could. Although He could see it all, I attempted to hide my idols from the Lord, and I fought to continue the hard
74

way, which seemed easy until my burdens became too much to bear.

Jesus yearned to take me much deeper with Him. I was still in lukewarm, sandy, muddled waters, walking back to the old, rather than letting go and walking into the new. I was, and I still am, a work in progress. But even then, I was still His beautiful masterpiece, and He was not about to let me go. He saw far more than I could see, and He never left my side. I was and am His child.

I did not know I could be free. I did not know I could let it all go and give it to Him. I had yet to discover my true identity in Christ, which He established before I was born on Earth. When I understood this after undergoing a process of change, I would be awakened to the truth that set me free.

It would take being caught in several riptides to lift my arms to the one who had been with me all along, just waiting for me to surrender in the mist of rough waters and to cry out to Jesus to rescue me. I simply was drifting and sinking as I clung to those idols and tried to do it myself rather than let Him do what He wanted to do using me!

How did I allow this? Well, simply by doing things the same way over and over! I used the do-it-yourself quick-fix method that led to instant gratification. I had adopted strategies and mindsets to prevent myself from having to process what the Lord was attempting to show me!

I was also trying to outrun Him. God wanted to show me the mountains in my life that were holding me back from moving forward; He wanted me to allow Him to move them! These were the same mountains He had already moved in Heaven's time, but I wanted to bypass that track and run around them rather than let the waters rise around that sandbar I was stuck in and trust that He would not let me sink! Thus, I went in circles for many years. Imagine the exhaustion I felt. I could have just spoken for those mountains to move in the name of Jesus and believe, but I did not know that strategy at the time.

I also did not understand that He could even move those mountains, although I was raised to believe this. Perhaps my faith was being tested for purpose. Perhaps He wanted me to remember what I believed deep within in my heart. But I failed to see that I was in a vicious cycle. God was waiting on *me*. He wanted me to move in the right direction. He wanted to be first in my life.

＊＊＊

After I was done with my birthday meltdown, back to Tennessee I went for another week. I knew I had to stay away from the temptations in Atlanta, and I sought security and stability. I tended to find that being accountable to someone else typically kept me in line.

Another pattern of mine? Find a man rather than resting in the arms of Christ. I was becoming close with a male friend who worked out at my gym and lived nearby, and I decided that a relationship with him had to be the answer.

Looking back in retrospect, my motives were in no way pure for getting involved with my close male friend, who I did love spending time with, but mostly I did *not* like his attention on other girls! On top of the jealousy factor, I was desperate for approval and comfort after making bad decisions when intoxicated, and I saw him as a security blanket that would keep me away from the Atlanta party scene.

Initially, my friend was not interested in having a committed relationship with me, but I was determined to make that happen, although I was in no position to be involved in a relationship in the first place. In fact, I compromised some of my morals to gain his attention.

It seemed I had learned to enjoy the pain that came from forcing my way through doors that did not need to be opened. But I never thought ahead to the pain part. I just wanted to push the door open without stopping at the red lights along the way, regardless of what was in my way. I lacked awareness, and my decision-making skills were affected by self-destructive patterns.

Regardless, the friendship eventually *did* develop into a relationship. The relationship had ups and downs like most, but starting it off with lots of downs. He was unsure about what he wanted *(which I don't blame him for, given I was the one trying to force him into it!)* When I sensed this, I gravitated toward self-destructive patterns of the past. This led to more instability than the stability I originally sought.

Looking back, I see I had all the signals that I would be walking into something that would only lead to pain. I was building sandcastles on a sandbar that would get swept away by the incoming tide. Foolish is the man who builds a house on sand, right? One is not ready to build anything if he or she lacks the proper materials.

God still had major work to do on my heart. If one's motives are not based in love, someone loses. If God is not behind the door of a relationship, He can easily allow the door to close. What I was trying to build eventually fell to the ground. Today, I know that when we force open a closed door, it is only the devil attempting to deter and lure us in, hoping we will hurt someone and get hurt ourselves. God does not want us to receive the pain that comes through forcing our way into any situation. We must wait for affirmation from Him as to which door is the right one that will lead to gain. The right door in any relationship will require compromise, but it will not require compromising our love for the Lord.

———————————✺◦❦◦✺———————————

Down the line, when he *was* ready to give the relationship his all, but I was already gone; literally and figuratively. I moved home to Atlanta, hoping that I would find security in the familiar living with my family while I commuted for my final semester of graduate school. I had only one class left before graduation, and I was finishing my Master's thesis project. I was unhappy with some of my decisions related to my former relationship in Tennessee and wanted to forget about them, so I traveled home, focusing my efforts on interviewing with potential employers.

I had more time on my hands as I had resigned from my company and was no longer working full-time. Once again, my idle hands found their way back into the devil's workshop in the Atlanta party scene.

I had previously met someone in a restaurant, and we reconnected as soon as I moved back into town. Although he was very balanced and focused, he introduced me to a group of people who practically ran the nightlife scene in Atlanta. This social circle partied hard almost every day of the week. I was in no way used to that lifestyle, but I liked being part of the group, and I liked him. I constantly faced temptation after temptation when I was around some of his friends, although he seemed to know how to maintain order in his life and not get distracted. On the other hand, I did not know my limits.

Just as we began dating, he quickly stepped in and make it clear that he would have no tolerance for my lack of control while out on the town. It was not that he was controlling; he simply did not want to be with a party girl. At the time, I was not capable of holding myself accountable, but I believe God used him to help me work towards this. As we moved forward from casually dating into a relationship, I was forced to choose to continue with my usual patterns or have a relationship with an amazing man I deeply respected. I chose the relationship, as I had learned from my past. I loved him very much, I was very happy, and I maintained balance in my life during this relationship as it meant more to me than partying or things that served no real benefit in my life. I followed his lead simply because I wanted to follow him as a leader. My parents also highly respected him, and I valued their opinion as well in terms of my choices in relationships. The Lord certainly used him to protect me from the distractions I had fallen prey to in the past.

As our relationship continued, I graduated at the top of my class, I was the student who was chosen to receive the annual award given for success both in academia and work in my field, and I landed my dream job in Atlanta at the same consulting firm in which I had wandered past the day I got off on the wrong floor when running late for work! *Coincidence? I think not!*

I was very happy and successful in my new position. However, my boyfriend accepted a position in another state a few months later. This move was best for him, and I understood. I was too fond of my organization and role to consider leaving, but that did not prevent me from lamenting that I would not be near my boyfriend. Regardless, we managed to see each other almost every weekend despite the 12-hour distance.

Typically, he would fly in late each Friday night and take the early am return flight home every Monday morning. If not, I would leave Atlanta Friday night to visit him and return at the crack of dawn and immediately head to my office from the airport at the start of the work week. Our weekends typically consisted of going out on the town with friends Friday evening, relaxing with my family Saturday afternoon, visiting his family that night, spending the day with them Sunday, occasionally going to church, and rising at 3:30am on Monday morning to go to the airport.

Looking back, I see God used this long-distance relationship in attempts to anchor me and to draw me closer to Him. I also believe He wanted me to stay focused on my work rather than getting too distracted with others. I was living at home with my family and had much time to focus on the Lord, but I began to miss my boyfriend to the point that I felt empty without him. We had spent so much time together before his move. I had forgotten what to do with myself when I was alone. Fortunately, the last thing I wanted to do was cause friction in my romantic relationship by spending time with people who had not been constructive in my past.

I missed him more and more each day. I was very sad and started hinting to him that I should be there with

80

him and we should get engaged, knowing that I would not be willing to leave my new job unless it was well worth it—meaning a proposal. He told me it was not time for me to live with him, as he was busy getting things settled and in place. I tried my best to be patient, but it was hard to keep my feelings to myself. He began to get frustrated and stressed with my promptings related to an engagement, especially because he was also in a new position and handling important family affairs.

One day, he made it clear that marriage was not a part of his plan for several more years. I will never forget his words, which he said with a smile and good intentions, "I am not getting married before 30, and one day, you will thank me when you are 30 and still single." At the time, I was 23 years old.

He was right, and I *did* get the opportunity to thank him when I was 30 and still single. I was not ready for marriage. The Lord still had a lot of work to do before He was going to show me the person he set aside for me. His timing is the perfect timing, and I have learned to wait and be patient.

At the time, not only was I not ready, but I was very impatient. I was very much in love and could not stand the distance between us. How would I do this for seven more years? I started to become depressed, finding myself crying myself to sleep. I felt there was a huge void I did not know how to fill during the week when we were not together. I was lonely at my parent's home, and the money I would have spent towards my own place was going towards plane tickets. I began to resent my boyfriend for this.

I started to get weary of the long weekends while he was in town and the sulking over missing him before he even left to fly back home. I found myself getting agitated while he was in town, resenting that he did not "want me" with him permanently. How would we continue this long-distance relationship with constant travel?

My resentment turned into bitterness when I saw him from that point forward. I attempted to turn off my feelings as I felt rejected. It just seemed too hard, and I did not think I could handle the pain I was experiencing much longer. I began to emotionally give up, playing pretend that everything was fine. I wanted it to be, but it just wasn't. There was a void in my heart that I did not know how to fill. I was lonely and unhappy. I desired affection and attention. My boyfriend simply could not give me what I wanted, although I know he cared.

One Friday evening, I refused to simply "stay in and do nothing" when he could not come in town. I went out with a close girlfriend who was trying to set me up with someone, but I told her there was no way I would have eyes for another man. I firmly believed this, yet she insisted I would like him, and I insisted, "no." Although I was still uninterested in meeting him, I reluctantly agreed that we could go to the bar where he was with several friends after the two of us had a few drinks at her place. I just wanted to be social with my friend, but after a few too many drinks at her house, that's not how the night turned out.

When I met this individual, I was immediately drawn to him. He was a few years older than me, very successful, intelligent, charismatic, good-looking, athletic, and he also went to my church. *"Church? Wow! Someone who goes to church without me having to even ask?"* I thought to myself. He seemed

82

as if he was ready to settle down in life with the right person. I loved the attention he was giving me, and for the next few days, we were inseparable.

I had done a 360 in less than two weeks—I went from having a strong desire to get more commitment from my boyfriend, to being completely emotionally numb, to having intense feelings for someone else.

Feelings often lie to us, and the devil often uses red shiny apples to deceive and then ensnare us, telling us it will make us "feel" better. Those apples look so great—as if they are the solution to all our problems—but they are often attempts to kill, steal, or destroy—no matter how long it takes. They are trap doors. We must remember than appearances can be deceiving.

I remember the day I opened the door and saw my boyfriend crying. We had been at the pool earlier in the day, and while he was cleaning off in another room, I texted my new fling. My boyfriend had sensed I was distracted for most of the day. He knew *something* was wrong. I quickly deleted the text before he came back in the room. When it was my turn to rinse off from the pool, my fling returned my text. I had not thought that far ahead, and my boyfriend saw the text while I was in the other room.

When I told him the truth, he told me he was planning on asking me to move in with him the next time he visited. He was too late. I was too early. Either way, it was not meant to be, and it was over—and over in a very messy way.

I was numb and did allow myself to feel pain at this point in my life. What I had done to hurt him did not hurt because I had taught myself to not feel hurt in general. Instead, I ran in fear to the arms of someone who I barely knew. Ultimately, this decision led to a downward spiral…along several flights of stairs.

———————————————————

I have forgiven myself, but I later went through a lot of pain before the healing. God used this to help prepare me for the man He ordained for me. It showed me the value of trust and respect, and I learned more about the traits I need to look for in someone to have a successful marriage.

———————————————————

I had walked right into another "relationship" while carrying the baggage of my past that I had yet to open, sort through, and decide what I wanted to trash. I did not know what was inside, because I failed to examine my heart. Instead, I had lined myself up with someone who did not love me and used words that hurt me deeply. The devil used that as ammunition to cause depression and anxiety.

I began to believe the lies of the enemy as this new man began to point out every "imperfection" of mine—lies that told me I needed a nicer car—nicer clothes—more money—more education—straighter teeth—a stricter bedtime—to be worthy of him. I began to feel *less than* and that being *me* was not good enough. I had never viewed myself this way in my entire life, but as I continued to date this person, this is how I felt.

I started to feel I had to change who I was to meet criteria that I did not want to fit in the first place. After he highly suggested I continue with my studies, I decided to start an online Ph.D. program in Organizational Psychology while working as an external consultant, although that was not something I wanted to do nor felt I needed to do. However, the words he used caused me to believe that I needed to be a doctor to be good enough—to be "at his level."

I felt controlled by someone who seemed great on paper, but I clearly saw his intentions were not right. Things were not as they had first appeared. I was frustrated, and I became vulnerable. I had rushed into dating someone new to escape my pain. Perhaps the void I tried to fill was not to be filled by man, but by the Lord Himself, my first love and truest love of all!

I forgot that I was already sealed, stamped, and approved by the Kingdom of God and man's approval is meaningless! As a princess of the King of Kings, I am worthy, and I do not need certain material items or works to prove my worth to anyone! My worth is not determined by my position or what appears on paper or on the surface! God judges the heart, and my heart is His! I worship Him and Him alone, not man or the things of the world!

Today, I have forgiven myself for allowing the devil to use his words to cause me to feel I needed another degree to feel worthy when that degree was not something the Lord called me to at that time. This decision would be a major lesson down the road to listen to the words of Jesus speaking to my heart rather than be persuaded by what others "felt" that I should do. Like many others, I was once easily influenced by what the world told me to do, but the more intimacy we have with the Lord, the more we can hear Him speaking to our heart.

This relationship ended almost as quickly as it began. This man was not who God had set aside for me, but instead of letting go and accepting God had something better in mind for me, I felt condemned that I was not good enough for anyone. This man had made several comments about my addictive habits, and the devil lied to me, telling me that just because I had a struggle, I was unworthy of love from anyone. The Lord was using him to show me that I did have a struggle that certainly could affect my relationships and life in general, but instead of running to the Lord and allowing Him to wash me with grace, I sat in my hurt, pain, guilt, and condemnation.

By sitting in my fear, I was running from the Lord instead of running to him. In fact, I did not go to church the day after we broke up in fear that I might see him and feel more rejection. During that church service, I lingered at home in a deep depression that I had never experienced. I was in full-on panic attack mode.

The enemy's plan? To keep me out of the church, out of fellowship with other believers, and to fall deeper into my addiction, deceiving me that I had it under control and it was the only way that I would be able to meet men and have fun with my friends. He knew that my drinking typically led to bad decisions, depression, and anxiety. His plan was to make me hate myself.

Today, I know my authority in Christ, and do not let fear or mistakes of the past delay or hinder me from my calling. When God says, "Lyndsay, it's go time!" I trust His words that speak life! I reject the lies of the enemy!

But I did not grasp this revelation until later in my life. After this relationship, I allowed the devil to continue to plant seeds that led me further and further down the spiral staircase. Although this relationship was what I once called "the beginning of the end," meaning the beginning of my "bottom" with addiction and toxic relationship patterns, I now see this as the beginning of the end of one of the biggest struggles of my life as I am an Overcomer through Christ alone!

Despite my depression over relationship struggles, I will never forget the six last words this man I dated ironically spoke to me; valuable words which I will never forget: "Begin with the end in mind."

Today, I live in the moment with my eyes fixed on Christ, who knows my true purpose and destiny, but I also know the "hang-ups" that would have ended my life if Christ was not a gracious God with another plan that is "immeasurably more than all we ask or imagine, according to his power that is at work within us" (Ephesians 3:20)! I *know* who I am in Christ, I *know* I have eternal life in Him, and I *know* He tells me to walk in faith and let the Word be the lamp unto my feet and a light unto my path! I am a walking miracle, evidence of His miraculous power of redemption! I am a living testimony of His resurrection power!

I later understood that God used a demolition process of tearing down the old to transform me into the new. In my 20s, I was stuck on that sandbar attempting to build a house on sand rather than rock. However, as I surrendered to the process of letting the old go and allowing the Lord to teach me how to walk in faith, God rebuilt my life on a firm foundation, with Him as the Cornerstone. I now have an intimacy with the Lord which often requires being still and listening. This intimacy has allowed me to gain an understanding of the lessons of the past which I missed while stuck on that sandbar, thirsty for Living Water, yet unaware that it was just what I needed to fill all the voids I felt in my heart. But once I tasted and saw that it was good, I would never thirst again.

What a beautiful thing, when life takes us unexpected places, regardless of how bumpy the ride on the way to the destination.

Chapter Six: Driftwood Along the Shore

Go up into the mountains and bring down timber and build my house, so that I may take pleasure in it and be honored," says the LORD.
~Haggai 1:8

The demolition phase of tearing down the old had yet to begin. I found myself falling deeper and deeper into the traps of the world which resulted in falling deeper and deeper into bondage. I was forgetting who I was in the process, especially with not going to church or participating in my weekly women's small group.

Just like lilies in the valley, we need light—fellowship with other believers and intimacy with Christ; as well as living water—fresh outpourings of the Holy Spirit— to spiritually thrive.

Without being "watered," or receiving much ministering, I was becoming dry; I found myself landlocked. The seeds of those beautiful flowers the Lord had planted in my life were simply no longer receiving constant sunlight. The useless and destructive weeds were not being uprooted, preventing those flowers to fully bloom. In fact, the weeds were beginning to take over the foundation of my life.

I praise the Lord that He eventually took me through a unique healing process—one that was designed specifically for *me*. During this process, I developed a deeper intimacy with Christ, I discovered my true identity as a daughter of the King, and I learned to identify the weeds in my life that would reap no harvest. Once those deep-seated tangled weeds in my heart that once hindered me were uprooted, I saw that I had freedom in Christ, my past had been redeemed, and I was free to bloom as the unique flower I was made to be. I saw the beautiful rose I truly was with a new set of eyes; the eyes of my Maker.

This required clearing out the old pieces of rotten wood from the construction site before rebuilding my life on a foundation of solid rock. If one does not stand on something strong, he or she will eventually fall. The Lord allowed me to fall, but He also rescued me.

Yes, I was certainly drifting in the shallow water of life, away from His living water in the deep ocean, much like driftwood floating towards the shore. However, driftwood is seen by many as beautifully imperfect and useful for new things of value. As I continue with this chapter of my life, please keep in mind the beauty of driftwood once it soaks in water long enough. Broken pieces can become masterpieces in the eyes of Christ. God is an expert in the restoration business. His living water turns ashes into beauty. Once I soaked in living water, I saw the beauty in my weaknesses, which were constantly being refined by His grace and made perfect in His power.

I was broken at this point in my life. My drinking was now regularly paired with the use of stimulants. Parties typically turned into after-parties each weekend, and my house was often the designation, which opened the door to sexual sins with both men and women. In fact, during these years, I was deceived into believing I was bisexual. I renounced this later in life after realizing this lie stemmed from being deeply wounded by men in the past. I had experienced hurt, control, manipulation, and physical abuse, which caused me to crave attention from *anyone* who could make me feel safe and loved.

During those dark days, I often stayed up all night on Fridays and Saturdays, hating the sound of birds chirping in the morning after my social affairs of the previous evening continued into the early hours of the next day. I always started my nights out at a classy venue, where I was treated as a high-profile socialite. But after those that knew some level of moderation left the scene, I remained with those who wanted to continue to party. But even the "functioning" partiers fall at some point if they do not walk away, regardless of success, power, or money. I certainly had been "functioning" in my demise for several years. I am thankful the Lord allowed me to fall when I did, although it was a painful fall. For some, they fall when it is simply too late. Others fall and give up, never realizing God is the source of all hope. And others? Their lives are cut short. But my story? It is simply one of miracle after miracle; grace from God that I simply do not deserve.

Even though I was falling deeper into a pit, God saw me as His bride. I may have been perceived by those in certain circles as part of "the elite," but I was certainly not acting like the bride of Christ. The devil was using my associations to continue to pull me down. Deceived and misled, I was not only allowing this, but I was being used to pull down other women who followed my lead.

I have had to forgive myself for taking the positions of leadership God gave me in various areas of my life and squandering them by leading many of the women who saw me as a leader straight into the wilderness. I have had to forgive myself for being a prodigal child. And guess what? The Lord not only forgave me, but He welcomed me back with open arms. He treated me as His princess. He surrounded me with His love. This is what He longs to do for His prodigal children.

Yet during this time, I had jumped on the wrong ship and was headed in the wrong direction. It would be a long journey before I returned home—and an even longer time to realize I was on the wrong ship.

The ship route I was headed down opened doors to carrying additional cargo I was not made to carry, including anxiety. Thus, I sought a psychiatrist, who prescribed me Xanax for my panic attacks. I asked for this after being very disturbed after hearing some family news. However, I had become accustomed to quickly relying on anything that prevented me from processing any level of discomfort in life. Rather than using them as prescribed, Xanax became my quick-fix remedy to calm my heart after using stimulants all night.

I was not only drinking to cope with the pressures of life, but I was now taking one drug to keep me from getting sloppy drunk and another to numb myself once I woke up and felt shame and anxiety. Bottom line, I was not on a righteous path, and my spirit was beckoning me to turn around and run to The Prince of Peace, my Abba Father.

The mindsets I had slowly adopted while in bondage led to more poor choices regarding dating. I began to seek out men that would not put me down for excessive drinking. I began to choose to spend time with those who did not walk with God, pretend to, or even know Him. I dated men who had faced defeat and turned to drugs. But they did not serve my needs either; I was simply lowering my standards.

Choosing to align myself with the wrong men caused more issues. One night while on vacation, I was raped by my boyfriend while I was asleep in our hotel room with my sister. I had taken it too far that night with drugs and alcohol and was out cold. My sister was fast asleep. My boyfriend also took that opportunity to run up hundreds on her credit card. Although the credit card situation was resolved, the whole ordeal put a strain on my relationship with my sister. She had not been a fan of this person from day one.

I was shocked at the reaction of this boyfriend of several months when my father intervened. My father was furious after I told him what happened while I was asleep. It was only the Holy Spirit that guarded my father's tongue and prevented him from responding in anger.

I ended the relationship immediately. However, the consequences of my poor choice in entering this relationship did not end at this point; it began to impact my living situation. While traveling for business up North a few weeks later, I started receiving phone calls that a man who identified himself as my boyfriend was lingering around my apartment complex. After returning from my business trip, I eventually contacted the police when I did not feel safe in my own home, where my sister and I lived.

I was embarrassed about my choice of jumping into something with someone so quickly without noticing the red flags my family seemed to see from the start. I did not notice them because I was in no place to at this point in my life. Even though I had a wonderful career and appeared polished and poised, my actions behind closed doors were a clear indication of the mess on the inside—within my heart.

I had a lot of forgiving to do, but the hardest part was forgiving myself.

Forgiving others as well as ourselves is the foundation to our healing, deliverance, and freedom. When we do not forgive, we leave ourselves vulnerable to being attacked by the enemy.

During this time, I could not forgive myself. I wanted to simply forget about it and pretend everything was okay! I wanted to keep on my mask.

Ironically, I remember walking into a venue one evening with two individuals literally wearing a mask per the theme of the social event. I had become involved in a twisted love triangle where I was intertwined with both individuals. News of this began to travel to my family, who was becoming concerned.

I ran. I accepted an invitation from an admirer to fly oversees with him for a business trip. I was very angry at the time, so I impulsively decided to go after setting boundaries that I was not interested in anything at a romantic level. However, I was fully aware that he wanted more than just friendship, despite his agreement that things could remain platonic given that was my wish.

I wanted to feel better, but I didn't. After the trip, I felt worse. Things did not go well when he could tell I was aloof. I drank excessively during the extravagant dinners to numb myself from experiencing my emotions. I am sure I did not act in my right mind, and

I know I was not always kind. I quickly realized I had not made the right decision to go on that trip while I was still processing unrelated prior events.

I was stuck in a pattern and did not realize that what I was feeling was conviction to turn around and let God lead me down His path. Instead, I felt shame that turned into blame. I knew better than to put myself in the position I was in, literally on the other side of the world with someone who had clearly expressed an interest in me. My heart knew I was not emotionally available in any way, and I was certainly not in a place to make rational decisions. On top of that, I could not control my drinking.

I was running to what I thought was an out, but only God could fill the void in my life. Yet He never stopped pursing me, despite how far I ran from Him.

Although the trip was chaotic at times, I spent many quiet, beautiful moments alone exploring the country. I cherished these moments of tranquilly.

One day, a driver was hired to take me anywhere I desired. I remember hearing my friend tell his driver to be sure to take me shopping—on his dollar—anywhere I would like. I chose the ocean. That was something I was not about to miss.

One of the most amazing moments of my life was jumping into the cold, beautiful ocean on the other side of the world, watching the surfers ride the waves. I literally Baywatch-style ran into the water, throwing my purse on the sandy shore along the way. I was more than ready to feel the rush of the salt water against my skin. As soon as the water was deep enough, I dove in, loving the rush of the waves crashing over me.

I felt wild. I felt free. I felt alive. I felt…me.

Today, I know it is vital to my being to choose to live life fully alive in Christ—to choose to accept and keep the freely given gift of joy, regardless of any circumstance!

As a young girl, I was filled with the joy of the Lord. I was also typically the first one to jump in the water, regardless if it was freezing. At times, I was often the only one to jump in during the rain or colder months of the year, but I loved the thrill. I loved the free feeling of being in the water. Today, although I likely am still one of the first to run into the ocean when the opportunity arises, the Lord has also taught me to test the waters when it comes to my choices regarding decisions, relationships, and opportunities.

Flying across the world at a drop of the hat while angry at a former boyfriend may have been a temporary attempt to distract and free myself from thinking about it, but it did not heal my pain from years of suffering in silence about certain relationships and experiences. That void could only be filled by my Healer, Jesus Christ.

Yes; what I was thirsty for was living water. This thirst could only be satiated by relishing in the fullness of Jesus Christ—by going deeper into the ocean of His love.

I needed it. I wanted it. Yet, I had forgotten the taste of it.

Years later, I did reestablish a beautiful level of

intimacy with Jesus that brought me deeper than ever before; He brought me into His inner chambers, where He allowed me to drink from the deep wells of water springing from a fountain of His love. While tasting from this living water fountain, I discovered true satisfaction in Jesus until my cup became full to the point of overflow. Here, in this inner chamber with Jesus, I discovered my true purpose in Him.

During these unsettling times, I was beginning to drown without even realizing I was growing tired as I latched on to anything or anyone that would hold me above the waves rather than run to Christ. I looked for things of this world to serve as my "lifesaver," rather than the Savior of my life—the One who saved me before I was even born by sending His son to die for me on the cross.

I was not at all concerned with my true direction or ultimate destiny. I figured I had time to veer outside the lines for a few more years! I was a typical Type-A driver who was driving in more than one lane. In fact, I was literally driving in the wrong lane after making a turn when I was pulled over and slapped with a DUI one rainy Thanksgiving night.

Jail was not fun, especially when you are used to taking medication for panic attacks and suddenly don't have them. I was terrified. I was mocked by the staff, who deemed me "Barbie." I certainly looked out of place in that holding area, dressed in my classy upscale designer clothing, perfectly done makeup, and long, blond hair. They told me that if I didn't stop crying and shaking, "being in the hospital handcuffed to a bed wouldn't be fun." At that point, I was so petrified that I wet my pants. True story! Fortunately, the women around me who were also in the holding area calmed me down, and I will forever be grateful for those ladies who the Lord used that night. He certainly can use anyone or anything anywhere to demonstrate He is with us.

Although God never left my side, this was the night He began to allow harsher consequences for my disobedience. This time, He gave me more than just a warning. He began to knock firmly on the door of my heart. Despite this, I did not listen. I considered the event a mere coincidence! I was not yet desperate enough to realize that I needed Him. I did not realize how thirsty I was, and what I was drinking was certainly not going to quench that thirst!

I had pushed my first love to the side, but He never forgot about me. He did allow me to get bounced around a bit in the waves so that I would reach out for His hand! He wanted me to remember that *He* is my true "life Savior"—my Redeemer who walks on water—the original blood donor Himself, Jesus Christ.

Today, I love walking in faith, holding hands with the One who holds me in His arms; my covering, regardless of where I am going. My loving Father is the umbrella of my life and the wind in my sails, regardless of any storm. Life is truly an adventure on His perfect path. It is one of beautiful mystery, fulfillment, and joy.

To think that at one point I thought it would be boring to be on the right path, as my curiosity and need for thrills was known to drag me toward the wrong places in the past, but I was wrong! Yes, the Lord gave me my curious nature for a reason, and I eventually learned to use this trait for His original purpose rather than allow the enemy to use it against me.

Don't you love how the Lord takes what the enemy meant for evil and turns it into good?

Yet on this path of destruction, I continued to encounter further loss. Weeks later, I totaled my car while texting a girlfriend about a photoshoot. My vehicle was destroyed. Then, I got scammed when purchasing a new car. Several thousand dollars later, the police could not do anything to recover the assets. I was the fool. I was still overly trusting and naïve, and I was filled with embarrassment about this, but I was in a position where I could purchase a brand-new convertible despite the hit. There still seemed to always be an easy-fix-it remedy to all my issues that did not require crying out to God in desperation.

I honestly did not understand what truly walking in faith was at this point, because I always found a solution on my own; at least what I *thought* was a solution.

But my life was filled with deception. I had problems making good decisions, I often acted in haste, and I certainly had yet to develop the gift of spiritual discernment. I could not distinguish between who was trustworthy and who was not, and I certainly could not discern what was sent from the Lord verses what came from the enemy. I had yet to learn that if something sounds too good to be true, it usually is, as appearances are often deceiving. Often, if the devil was holding out a shiny-red-apple-easy-way-out, I fell for it.

I was slowly discovering why the Word tells us to be *in* the world, but not *of* the world. The world was certainly not the loving, Christian environment in which I was raised. Fortunately, there are more for us than against us! Yet there was much more going on that my eyes could not see in another realm. *There was and is a spiritual battle going on; one that has already been won!*

For our struggle is not against flesh and blood, but against the rulers, against the authorities, against the powers of this dark world and against the spiritual forces of evil in the heavenly realms.
~Ephesians 6:12.

At one point in this battle, the devil attempted to steal much from me. However, the Lord eventually taught me how to fight the good fight and stand my ground with the authority I have been given as a Child of God. He taught me how to dust off my feet and continue to stand no matter what was in my path. Jesus put an end to all pain and hurt when He died on the cross for my sins. After true repentance and forgiveness, I am certain that the Lord commanded that the enemy to restore all that he stole seven-fold!

Thank you, Lord for this promise! Thank you, Lord, that our past does not determine our future because of your amazing grace and mercy! Thank you, Lord, that you restore the years that the cankerworm stole! Thank you, Lord, for victory, restitution, and turning everything around on the enemy because of the blood of Jesus! Nothing you allow is ever wasted! Your promises are true, and I stand on the Word of God; the way, the truth, and the light, which pierces all darkness! Thank you, Lord, that Your promises are true! Your love never fails!

How beautiful are the waves of the sea, gently tossing driftwood that has floated away from its home into the deep ocean, then perfectly placing them back to peaceful positions along the shore. The waves leave lasting unique imprints on each piece of driftwood only after the cleansing of the salt water. These are matchless treasures, with distinctive patterns that dance deep into each crevice after time spent soaking in the sea. During their journey, what may have appeared as being tossed and thrown about the waves was only a dance; a song of victory singing "return to sender." How beautiful it is when we fully embrace God's plan and learn to see the currents in life as a reason to praise the Lord, trusting He will complete the good work He began long ago! How beautiful are the melodies He sings over us. He whispers, "Let me be the wave. I know where I am sending you—back to me and where you will be free to be used mightily for me. Let's dance together as we travel to my perfect place."

Chapter Seven: Lighthouse for the Lost

"Because he loves me," says the Lord, "I will rescue him; I will protect him, for he acknowledges my name."
~Psalm 91:14

In case you have yet to figure out the protagonist of this book, it is Jesus Christ. Although I have a supporting role in the Kingdom of God, He is the one who supports me. He lives in me; I am but a willing vessel. During this chapter of my life, my self-worth was rooted in my professional and social prowess. God was certainly not the center of my life. My life was out of balance spiritually, despite the way things appeared.

For example, I was featured as one of the city's Most Eligible Bachelorettes in Atlanta's "Modern Luxury" Magazine during this time. My two-page write-up and picture headlined the featured article of the magazine that month. Looking back, I find the first words from the article detailing what made me so "eligible" quite ironic. They read, "Lyndsay Wrensen is determined to find balance in life." Today, well over ten years later, I have made great progress towards this goal. The key to balance is a life centered on God and His greatness. It is a physical, mental, and spiritual alignment centered on the Word of God. However, God is constantly at work in our lives, and sometimes, we need frequent adjustments.

The magazine teamed up with a well-known non-profit for a date auction, where men could "bid" to have a date with those featured in the article. I immediately hit the maximum "bid" of $1500. Yes, it went to a great cause, but God knew my light needed some changes before it could shine for *His* glory, rather than for *my* glory. He knew He had put more inside of me than merely how I appeared on the outside or "on paper." He knew the greatest gifts were still buried underneath a lot of clutter, diminishing the brightness of my light as a Child of God. Those are the gifts that are eternal and never fade.

As I continued to walk in my will, I was contacted by various reality TV shows. I was asked to host parties at lounges and clubs, model for various designers, and I was occasionally cast in commercials, short films, and voice-over roles. I was pulled into another dating auction with my sister. I began recording demo songs I wrote with producers for fun, but the words coming from my heart were not always a pleasing aroma to the Lord. I was accepted as a member of an exclusive group of women who sought to improve communities, promote volunteerism, and develop other women, but I also loved the exclusiveness that came with it—the upscale charity events, the dinner parties, and the gatherings. I wanted to impact society positively and make a difference, but I was still living a sinful unexemplary lifestyle behind the scenes. Not everything I did in attempts to be "on display" glorified God. They may have appeared to, but God is more concerned with the heart.

I still thought I was the one with all the strength.

But I was thriving, right? Climbing to the top, right? Too busy to "be still" right? Too successful to slow down and listen for direction! Too…prideful.

I was blinded by the lights.

My family, especially my father, could see this as well. They decided it was time for an intervention, and I mean an actual *intervention*. My best girlfriend picked me up from my office for "lunch" one afternoon, and when we pulled up to a building with a sign reading "Break Free," I was appalled. She talked me into walking in, but I was ready to dart. I was in no place to listen to the letters written by friends and family members who felt I was not the same person; those who stated addiction had a become a major issue within my life. I remember thinking to myself, *"I only do 'that' once or twice a month! There are people that do 'this' or 'that' every night! Doesn't my family have better things to do? Why is everyone on my case? And why did my friends come? They have their own set of issues!"*

I told my family and two friends who were invited to the meeting that I had clients to see and had to leave, and I demanded my best friend drive me back to my spacious office in Atlanta.

But my father was not about to let me go. As much as I wanted to push my family away, God placed me in the most perfect family for *me*. I love God's loving sense of humor. He gave me a loving father who was a psychologist and former lifeguard for a reason. He has the ability to see the signs of those who needed rescuing far in advance. Today, we both share that same gift, yet I had to first be willing to be rescued before I could learn how to rescue others.

When I failed to follow up for an appointment at the center, my father then attempted to reach me by emailing me a letter insisting that I get professional help to "deal with this in as civilized a manner as possible" and with the "least invasive approach." He was trying to be gentle, but he was fully aware that I

105

was playing defense, as evident in his email. But just like my loving Abba Father, he loved me too much to let me go. His email read:

Dear Lyndsay,

I think you know I would rather see you in jail, but alive, than to lose you to a life (however long or short) of alcohol/drugs/ etc. I spoke to dozens of people and "places" that provide help, and this was the most professional and workable from what I thought of what you needed and would accept…We've anticipated your objections and excuses regarding any plan we might develop. From what I can tell and from what I believe, your judgment is not what it could be, and your insight into what is happening is impaired. I see you on a road that will not lead you to your stated dreams, but rather a nightmare if this continues unchecked. Please don't think that I'm not prepared to take other steps to help rescue you from the deception and deceit that you appear to be getting sucked into. You are the "Perfect Storm" when it comes to the prototype or ideal for falling into this lifestyle…. attractive, available, some credentials, a nice job with nice prospects for the future...in an incredibly naïve, easily influenced and manipulated, and easily deceived container.

I know you must want this for yourself for anything positive to happen, and I really do not want to have to coax you or leverage things to try to get you to accept the help you need, but don't think you need, but understand that we're ready to do whatever we need to in order to keep you stay alive and retain what you almost seem to be recklessly throwing away. You've got a lot on the line right now if you are not aware and need to carefully consider your options, just as you did the night that I showed up at your Senior Prom. That night I asked you to "think very carefully and consider what you are doing" and that your decision would have "consequences way beyond tonight." You did think, and made the right decision, but weren't happy about it. Later you bragged to your friends about how much we loved you to show up at your prom. We "reclaimed" you then, and we're ready to do it again. Work with us. You have nothing to lose and everything to gain. You'll forever regret it and be angry at yourself if you don't accept the help that is in front of you. I asked you way back then to think and make the right choice, and I'm asking you again, ten years later.

Love,

Dad

But I failed to respond to his plea. Still in hopes that I would reschedule, my father sent me this letter:

Dear Lyndsay,

It comes as no surprise that you again felt the need to cancel your appointment…At this point it seems pretty clear to me as well as others that our attempts at getting you to acknowledge your problems and to encourage you to make a decision to address them didn't have much impact on you at all. I don't think you truly appreciate how off track you are and the seriousness of your situation and it's so difficult to watch you go further and further downhill. I won't pretend to be impressed with your stated intentions as to how you're going to change, nor to listen to how we shouldn't worry because you make good decisions, etc. I'm not sure that I see any clear changes at all since we met with you at Break Free and you're unwilling to accept the offer of help that those who love you have extended. You've distanced yourself from our family with your behavior and have chosen to continue along your path while making passing comments of how you're changing so as to create the illusion of reform…It comes as no surprise that you again felt the need to cancel your appointment. I wish you could see what this is doing to your future and how this impacts family relationships. Until you acknowledge how this is destroying you, your relationships, and robbing you of what you could have had…Until you are willing to make necessary changes, nothing will change for the better. It will be just one drama after another. Please let me know when you are willing to accept help or how you've made changes. So too, please understand it's difficult to be interested in other events, activities, situations you may be experiencing when this is at the forefront of my thoughts.

Love,

Dad

As I continued to reject the guidance from those God was using in my life to reach me and urge me to stop heading down the wrong path, I was headed downhill quick. And I literally mean *downhill*. Thankfully, fully aware of the steps I would soon take, God had a plan in mind to get my attention and save me from myself.

One evening, I rushed back from a dinner date to have a quiet evening with a close friend who was in town whom I was eager to see. We decided to meet at my condo and then grab a drink or two at a local hangout within walking distance from my condo.

The two drinks I had were more than potent; they were certainly too strong for me to handle. After stumbling home, I was not ready for the evening to conclude; I was ready for it to just get started. I made a few calls, and soon enough a few friends turned into more than just a few, including the DJ from the "latest and greatest" club—spinning live in my own living room.

In attempts to hear above the uproar, I pushed my way through the tiny living room to the back porch after receiving a call from a very close friend, Ryan, who had been in the hospital with leukemia for several weeks. I shut the door behind me and leaned over the edge of the corner of the back deck of my condo, desperately trying to make out what he was saying over the noise coming from both my living room and the loud outdoor AC unit to my left. As I was leaning over, I dropped my phone off the ledge.

Eager to speak with Ryan to continue the conversation and rather emotional and dramatic as I was intoxicated, I searched for a way to locate my phone immediately rather than waiting until daylight per the suggestion of others. Although it was pitch black in the dark woods beneath my deck and certainly a long way down, with a flashlight, I could easily see where my phone had landed—directly

109

below where I had been standing on the porch. If I could only find a way to get to it.

Although I was holding a flashlight, I was not seeing clearly in any capacity. I was not sober-minded enough to hear the still, small voice of the Lord, the true light, beckoning me to let it go for now—I never was after I consumed alcohol. Thus, I left my condo to take the elevator down to the main parking level. I walked to the edge of the concrete parking deck, peered down, and I reasoned I could easily hop over the ledge and walk to where the phone was about 30-feet away. The friend that followed me urged me to let it go, but I demanded he simply hold the flashlight from the ledge and drop it down to me once I was on ground level. I would then use it to locate the phone. I wanted to do it myself, right then and there. I did not need anyone helping me. *I was invincible, right?*

I climbed over the ledge, looked down, and my eyes perceived about a six-foot drop to the ground; slightly more than I would have guessed, but I remember thinking, "I can do this. It's only six feet!" Yup; I wanted to do things my way.

"Let me be the light, my Child. Let me be your guide. Do not take this into your own hands."

The last words I heard were, "Lyndsay, don't let go." I smiled, ready for the rush, and I let go. It was almost as if I could not control myself from this action. Whatever told me to let go was not in any way coming from God. I remember feeling overtaken by something—something almost evil—telling me to let go. Of course, this likely had a lot to do with the substances in my body, but I also sensed something else. I will never forget that moment. It was like I could

110

see myself from an outside view, and I simply was not in my right mind.

Yes, I was intoxicated, but I believe there was more going on at this moment. The morning before the night of that party, on that same balcony where I dropped my phone, I had been playing a game—a game my mother had told me since childhood to *never* play.

I had stayed up all night with two friends with whom I was doing drugs, and somehow the idea of playing Ouija Board popped in my mind. I remember playing it alone at one point when they stepped inside, and it was almost as if I was being drawn in, unable to stop. At that point, while under the influence of substances, I had opened another doorway to the enemy to cause further bondage. I praise Jesus for delivering me from my rebellious ways in the years to come, teaching me to renounce those actions and the words I may have spoken, forgiving me, closing that door, removing the darkness I had allowed in, and filling those areas with His light and love!

But that night, deceived by the darkness and thick overgrown ivy which was covering the *actual* height of the drop, I did in fact, "let go" and fall into bondage— bondage that left a cast on my foot for several months. Yes, I "fell" off what we estimated to be a 25-foot ledge. Although I did not hear or sense the Lord in the moment, He was right there. Holding me. Loving me. Embracing me. Alive in me.

"I love you at your darkest. It is I who catches you when you stumble. My light in you pierces all darkness. It is under your feet, child! You are mine! I am your Deliverer! You will live victoriously once again, child! I will awaken you!"

Despite being very intoxicated and numbed from the actual intensity of the pain, it more than just hurt when I landed, but I crawled to get the cell phone. I could not get back to where I had landed on my own; the friend who had urged me not to let go leaped down to my rescue, breaking his toe along the way. He carried me back to my condo.

"Daughter, it is I who will carry you through this storm. I am the Great I Am."

When I woke up in the morning, I was immediately taken to the ER with another friend who had stayed near my side to make sure I kept ice on my swollen foot. At that point, my foot had doubled in size.

"Child, I will never let you go. I will renew your strength because I love you! You have fallen, but it is I who will lift you up!"

Quickly after I arrived at the hospital, I was moved into another room, where I had surgery on my talus, apparently one of the three hardest bones to break in the body as well as one of the toughest bones to heal. It is taken seriously when this bone breaks, as this bone pivots the foot. The healing process is typically not a quick one. And the pain? Unbelievable. I was told I might never run again, but I praise the Lord that I am more than able to run, skip, and dance with Him side-by-side!

"I will heal every wound. I will heal every hurt in your heart. I will bind up your wounds as you surrender to me and my process. You will see this in time, my sweet daughter!"

Yes, the healing process would take time. After surgery, I laid on my couch in that same living room in complete pain. Instead of healing and laying low, friends came over to bring me casseroles. I took extra pain medication I was not prescribed and drank plenty of liquids (i.e., wine). Soon enough, I was back at work, but still at play, regardless of my cast and crutches, which I would have for several more months. I did not want to miss out on the party although I was injured. I knew no other way to live. To maintain my socialite status, I went everywhere with one heel, including clubs and bars.

"The medicine you need is found in embracing my love for you as The Healer, my dear one. Please don't fight me on this, child. I know best. Rest in me. I urge you to rest in me. Looking forward to that time. Waiting on you. I love you, my sweet daughter!"

A close girlfriend who had just relocated back to Atlanta moved in with me temporarily to help me get around my place in a wheelchair for a few weeks. I would have never made it through that time without her, and the Lord knew I needed a shoulder to lean on, literally. Yet the memory of the fall at my condo began to haunt me, so when my lease ended, I moved to another part of the city with a girlfriend. The Lord was opening the door for a fresh new start, but I was not ready to walk the narrow path.

After unpacking my things, two friends told me they had a surprise for me after they heard I was down one evening. The surprise? They wanted to set me up with someone. I was in no way interested. Although they were kidding in attempts to cheer me up, they begged me to look at his picture. When I finally did, my eyes lit up, half from shock, and half from curiosity—a personality trait the devil often tried to use to reel me in to a trap.

"Only I can fill that void you feel, child! That hole you feel inside your heart was made for only me!"

The picture was not of a "he." It was a "she;" an attractive, smiling blond girl with large brown eyes. And her name? I will call her "Lia" for her privacy. She openly identified herself as a lesbian; a lifestyle with which I was not familiar. My friends giggled and mentioned that they wanted to "set us up," and I immediately asked them what Lia was doing that evening. They had no idea I would take them up on their "offer," which was their attempt to uplift my spirits and see me smile, knowing I had once stated I was "bisexual." Perhaps they thought I would cheer up rather than stay alone in my room sulking.

But I was seeking a pick-me-up and desperate to go out and drink to numb the pain I felt on the inside of my heart, and the devil knew I was in a weak place spiritually, physically, and emotionally. I was seeking attention and very needy. My friends were staying in that night, but when I discovered Lia was out at local bars in my new neighborhood, I urged my friends to contact her. Perhaps I would accompany her and her friends as they ventured in this unfamiliar scene…into the unknown.

The girls agreed to make the call, as they knew the group and trusted I would be safe with them. Lia agreed to come over to my new apartment along with my two girlfriends, and I downed a drink while awaiting her arrival. I remember thinking, *"After a few drinks, I could play that role! Why not? My friends even support it! This should be fun! And who knows what could happen? You don't know unless you try it, right?"*

I was deceived. But God had a plan to use her in my life in a life-changing way down the line.

"This is a trap, my child. Do not listen to the lies of the enemy, my dearest! This is a carefully planned snare of the enemy set out to destroy you! That is his plan!"

When they arrived, Lia was fun, laid-back, funny, friendly, and very personable. I was immediately drawn towards her. I loved the attention she was giving me and felt safe. Although I had a broken leg, I trusted she would look out for me if I went out with them that evening. I knew I needed someone to look after me when I drank, especially with a cast.

"It is I who is looking out for you, my child, as I have since you were born. I am your Great Protector; press into me! You are safest in my will! Follow my path! You know the way to find this path. I will remind you. I will teach you to be still and hear my voice."

The following night, Lia and I met up again; this time, just the two of us. I slipped on a hardwood floor at a friend's house while using my crutches—again, intoxicated. When I fell, I put all the weight on my left wrist in attempts to protect my left foot. Lia took me to the hospital, and I was told I had a broken left wrist and that I needed to see a specialist immediately. The following morning, I saw a doctor who worked in the same practice as the orthopedic surgeon who was treating my broken foot.

"Please, child. Please listen to me. I want to save you from yourself. Make room for me. I love you."

I vaguely remember the doctor asking why I kept having injuries. I tried to play it off as an accident, although I knew it was due to being intoxicated. I tried to discount the alcohol factor, but the doctor saw straight through it. He scheduled surgery early the next morning and instructed me to not drink on the medication. I had hinted that it was the day before my birthday and the weekend of Halloween, and without giving him details, he was on to my plan and the potential wreckage it could cause.

The next day, I immediately went into surgery as planned, where a metal plate was placed in my left wrist to compliment the metal screws in my left foot. I came home in my wheelchair, now with two broken limbs—both on the left side of my body. *Have I mentioned I am left-handed?*

After sleeping off the anesthesia, my biggest concern at the time was not the pain; I was an expert at numbing pain of any type at this point. My biggest concern was also not how this would work at the office. My concern was how I would bathe and get ready by myself for my birthday event that evening. I was expecting about 50 people dressed in costume at a venue for my special day. Furthermore, I had a close friend flying in to see me as well. I did not want to disappoint anyone; I cared more about getting approval from others and having "fun" rather than allowing God to take His rightful place in the center of my life. Instead, I called a friend to ask her if I could swing by to pick her up so we could get ready together. On the way to get her, I complained about not being able to fit my arm through my costume.

"Rest in me. Be still, my child! Make room for me."

116

My girlfriend came to my "rescue," and I managed to find another costume in my closet (one of many back-ups) that I felt worked perfectly. My other friend flying in town arrived safely to the airport and came to my place, insisting he would carry me to dinner if he had to, but he did not think it was wise to go elsewhere. This dear friend had been with me earlier that year when my appendix almost ruptured and had urged me to go to the hospital. Had I not followed his advice, it could have been a disaster. When my appendix was removed, the doctors had found a small tumor inside the fleshly matter. It had been the first of three surgeries that year. The Lord certainly used him to signal me that I needed help that evening for a physical issue, but at this point, I failed to listen to anyone He was sending my way to assist me with the other issues in my life that needed immediate attention. Pride was in the way, and I was not willing to let go of it.

"I must teach you humility, my child. Without this, you cannot complete the good work I began long ago…and you cannot do it without me…"

I had shirked off the instructions of my friend and doctor, not to mention the pleas of my family, especially my father, beckoning me to lay low that evening. *Lay low?* That was something I did not know how to do.

My two friends and I headed to the event after a glass of champagne, where numerous friends would be gathered, including the members of my new Bible study group. When we arrived, I am sure the members of my small group saw straight through my attempt to hide my party lifestyle. However, they remained loving and completely non-judgmental.

117

In the meantime, my mind wandered to the one person who I knew would not be coming, Lia. I was already becoming completely co-dependent on Lia, and although I had just met her, I felt somewhat rejected that she had decided to continue with her original plans instead of attending my birthday gathering.

The plan was to go to the dinner gathering, then my close male friend who was visiting would bring me back to my place to rest. He urged me to limit my alcohol to no more than two drinks, but once we arrived at the dinner, my decision to follow those guidelines went out the window. As I continued to drink behind my friend's back, I decided to make my own plans. I snuck away from everyone, called Lia, ditched my wheelchair, grabbed one crutch, jumped in a taxi, and ventured back to the "unknown."

Lia was at her usual spot, where we had received so much attention a few nights before simply because we were two attractive blondes in a bar that was 99% full of male patrons. I had soaked up that attention. Years ago, I thrived on it.

"Child, your worth is found in me! You have my full attention! You do not need the approval of man! Come home; rest in my arms."

I saw only a glimpse of Lia before I heard the words that tore deep into my heart: *"Gimp!"* Who had called me a gimp? I noticed a girl I did not know standing near Lia, and I was filled with jealousy, hurt, and anger. I was drunk, and I became hysterical. I jumped back into the taxi, tears streaming down my cheeks, and I decided it was, in fact, time to go home. All I

118

wanted was to be alone in my bed, where I could cry with no one seeing.

"My grace is sufficient for you. My power is made perfect in weakness, child."

But when I finally decided to go home, where I planned on sulking in my self-pity, I found my apartment unlocked, and I was not alone. My close girlfriend whom I had picked up earlier was there alone with a male "friend" whom I often reached out to when I felt I needed additional medicine for pain. I was intoxicated and wanted to be alone, so I asked them to leave immediately. However, things did not move as quickly as I wanted. As I had picked my friend up earlier, she had no way home, but I did not care. At that moment, all I felt was hurt and rejected—my mind clouded by substances, and I simply could not handle any adversity.

"Child, I am your refuge. I am your lighthouse in the darkness. You carry that light within you, but your vision is blurred by the deception of the enemy. You have parked yourself in the enemy's camps, but I will rescue you. You may not see the light, but I do. In time, when you are ready, I will begin to teach you how see through the darkness with my eyes and guide others along my path. Yes, I will give you a new set of eyes. Surrender. I do not want you experiencing any additional pain. You are walking in your own will, yet you are deceived. I will break off all deception, my daughter!"

The next thing I knew, things began to escalate. I said something ruthless to my friend that she did not deserve. Hurt from my verbal blow, she responded in anger, and I retaliated. Moments later, my male "friend" frantically searched for my pills from surgery.

I somehow managed to get in my room alone with two broken limbs, lock the door, and call the police.

"There are more for you than against you. I am the Judge. You will teach my precious daughters their worth in me using you after I show you yours, My Princess."

The police did come that night. Fortunately, down the line, my female friend showed me grace for my part in the altercation and there were no legal repercussions.

I have forgiven myself for introducing her and others to a lifestyle that they did not know until they met me. Today, it is my prayer to be an influencer who turns others to Christ, rather to the ways of the world, despite my imperfections.

After the police left, escorting out my girlfriend as well as the person who sold pain pills, I crawled into my bed and called Lia, who came to my place to clean up the spilled wine that covered the hardwood floors. However, the real mess? *Me.* Thank goodness the Lord is an expert in the restoration business!

"You are covered in the blood of Christ, child! What you see as a mess, I see as a mechanism for my message of truth and my resurrection power! I see with eternal eyes! I make all things new. I will complete the good work I have begun, and it will be used for my glory!"

I felt safe for a moment after Lia arrived, thinking that the void I felt on the inside was at last filled. But when

I woke up in the morning, Lia had gone to work, and I panicked, thinking that I pushed her away due to my behavior. *What had I done? What had I become?* I was filled with guilt and shame. I felt disgusting…rejected…I felt empty. I felt alone.

"My spirit resides within you, my child! Look to me, daughter of the King! Come to me with all your burdens and weariness! I am here with you! You are not alone! I have never left your side! I am the only one who can fill that void. You will see! I love you, my daughter…my love for you knows no limits or conditions!"

As I lay there feeling helpless and all alone, I experienced a panic attack like no other. My roommate was at a friend's place, and as I laid in bed with a broken arm, a broken leg, a dead cell phone with no charger, a failed Internet connection on my laptop, and no way to contact the outside world, I wondered for a moment if perhaps God was trying to get my attention.

Yes, that is what it took.

"Child, I will do anything to have your attention, because I know what is best for you! I will have nothing less than the best for you! I want you to know me, not just know about me, as you did when you were young. I love you! I will never leave you, Lyndsay. You are my precious one. You are my Esther. I will redeem you. I see so much that you cannot yet see, and I cannot wait to open your eyes. Yes, I created you as a warrior for a purpose; a purpose that will be used for my glory. I will train you when you are ready to use your sword. Still waiting on you…Know that you will be what I say you will be!"

God had me just where He wanted me. And He had a beautiful plan. A plan to bring me home, just as He does for all His prodigal children.

Thankfully, I finally submitted to my family's plan and went to a facility that day, fully aware that I needed help. What a joy I must have been while I was there, with nurses having to take me to the geriatric unit to bathe in the handicapped shower due to my injuries. Seven days later, I left the detox unit I was in, oblivious that I had been there for alcohol abuse (which had been paired with pain medication), and my leg cast was immediately removed. Soon after, my arm cast was removed as well.

Yet I continued to drink. I had yet to be learn to be still and hear God's voice—the light in the darkness—my lighthouse—my safe-haven. I was looking for safety in the wrong places. It would take more to get my attention for longer than just a fleeting moment. And it would take even more to keep it. He was waiting for me to see that He was the only one that could mend all my wounds, heal all my pain, and fill the void that I continued to feel.

Thus, I continued to search in the wrong places, outside of the will of God. I decided that the answer must certainly be Lia. Before I knew it, my co-dependence with Lia had turned into a relationship, although I knew I was not a lesbian. Although being in this relationship was my solution and plan rather than the Lord's plan for my life, God used her to help set me on a narrow and righteous path. The Lord has a beautiful way of turning the enemy's plan against him to reveal His power for His Kingdom!

Lia admitted she thought my behavior was crazy when I drank, which was often the case, but she somehow saw my heart despite my personal issues. She was kind and attentive to my needs. I had no support from my parents in this relationship, and those I loved deeply often joked about it in disgust. They said they were kidding, but the hurt I felt from the comments only fueled me to pull away from them further.

Lia was always with me, and my roommate did not support it, so things began to get uncomfortable at our apartment. I felt Lia was the only one who cared about me.

One night, my roommate and I had a verbal conversation that ended our friendship of many years. She made a remark to me that cut deep. I lashed out at her in retaliation with a comment that cut even deeper. Things were not the same from that point forward. The relationship was severed. To this day, I have not had the opportunity to speak with her, although I do wish her the best.

About that time, my father wrote me another letter he titled, "Two Roads...Your Choice":

> Dear Lyndsay,
>
> I can so easily picture you in a nice business suit on a stage with a microphone speaking to a group of 500 people, sharing your testimony and letting others know how you finally got to the point of nearly losing it all, but making the courageous decision to invest the necessary time to seriously tackle your problems and stop the repeating pattern of crises, and to emerge as a confident and inspiring woman

who can positively impact the lives of others and save lives.

I can also, unfortunately, picture you in a hospital ward bed, with soft food clinging to the bib you are wearing, with an orderly wiping the drool from your mouth, trying to determine if you would like to take a sip of water, while you are making hard to distinguish grunts and moans, all this necessitated by having made one poor decision that stole the plan that the Lord had for you all along.

It's your choice. Please think, pray, and listen, and I'm sure you'll make the right choice. We have confidence in you, but it will require changes in your thoughts, behavior, and attitude.

Love,

Dad

Although this letter showed the deep concern of my parents, it did not make a dent. Later, my father sent me another letter, a revised version of "Two Roads":

Dear Lyndsay,

Your "luck" is going to run out sometime... maybe in a year, two months, or perhaps, tomorrow. So far, you've been very fortunate, or rather, God has protected you and shielded you from so many tragedies that could have come your way. He opted to allow you to be spared some things you deserve from having made poor choices. He has, though, given you numerous nudges and opportunities to turn from some lifestyle choices and turn toward Him, but you've barely listened or just listened for a bit. He's not going to give up, but it will, at some point, mean that He will allow you to experience the consequences of actions so you can realize what you're doing and turn to Him. He just keeps on knocking harder. I'm trying to help you listen to the signs He's sending you and trying to warn you before that moment comes. There's time for choices now. Later, your options will be reduced or eliminated.

When I first began writing this letter two or three months ago, I thought that it was fair to say you were at a crossroad and that you were struggling to choose the "right" road. At that time, I typed the following:

"There are two roads before you. Along one road will be all sorts of enticing detours that will provide excitement for the moment. You'll be seduced with promises of fame, pleasure, and attention. You'll encounter all sorts of lost and struggling people along this road. They'll certainly not be helpful people to have near you if your goal is to accomplish anything worthwhile and be fulfilled. This road will pull you deeper into alcohol and drug addiction and everything that goes along with it. Most likely you'll eventually be criminally charged with possession of an illegal substance, get a repeat DUI/DWI or hurt someone while driving…. Who knows, but it'll eventually lead to jail or some other limit of your personal freedom that you are taking for granted right now.

It could take a different form by way of disease, injury, or poor health. You could lose your job/profession and have little or no means of predictable income or will otherwise have to rely on someone else along with the strings attached. You'll lose hold of other values you've learned, will find it harder to make good choices, will become even more and more estranged from family, spend less time with them, will rely on chasing windmills for your fame, your personality/behavior will continue to change for the worst, and you'll find it more difficult to like yourself. Eventually, you may ultimately realize that you've made tragic mistakes.

I've met a lot of people who have chosen this road. The worst thing about this road is that it leads you to another ultimate destination, and it's not Heaven.

The typography of the other road is much different. It is the road that the Lord has for you that is not without its bumps, but it takes you to your ultimate destination and it ensures your safety. It is the road that brings you to all the Lord has for you. Along this road you'll find rest areas, those that want to help you when in need, a path of true and enduring happiness. It provides you with the constant assurance that you're on the right road, despite it sometimes seeming like a long journey. It is the road that protects us from ourselves and our selfish desires. The map for this road is the Bible, with a detailed listing of obstacles along the way that we can certainly avoid if we pay attention."

I hadn't written more than that as of two or three months ago. Now I would say you've already chosen the first road, knowing that the other road exists and where it leads. I also think, however, that you're glancing back at the other road, and you intuitively know that you need to get back on it. It's hard though because there are so many exciting and enticing things that have pulled you onto road number one and keep you there.

Lyndsay, Satan is the one who is putting those very enticing things before you on the road because he knows exactly what'll pull you and keep you there. Still, the Lord is calling you to turn around, drive back, and get on the right road, the only true road to travel. Please turn around before it's too late Lyndsay.

I don't think you can do it by yourself. In fact, I know you can't, but you're not willing to admit it, at least not now. I'm sure it'll be easier to admit it when we're visiting you someplace other than your apartment. It's very clear to see the path of destruction you're on. It affects not only you, but those you leave along the way, and the list keeps growing.

We love you Lyndsay, and it breaks our heart to see you doing this to yourself, throwing away what you've been given, while maintaining this "I've got it all under control" attitude. I know you think we must be clueless, old-fashioned, out-of-touch, holding onto some "old person out-of-date" thing.

Even if you don't want to look at this from a spiritual point of view, even someone who doesn't believe in God would be able to discern how personally destructive you've become, would be able to see your poor choices, and how much you've changed. You are not able to keep the majority of the plans you make with your family, consistently breaking them because of some "event" or calamity which likely comes from your other lifestyle choices. The explanations and excuses become more frequent, more anticipated, and more elaborate. Clearly, this wouldn't be occurring if you were making better choices in your life. I'm not saying you are not smart Lyndsay. I'm just saying it's not doing you much good at all. It'll do you little good to ultimately get your Ph.D. and be unemployable in any capacity. It doesn't do any good to know what you should be doing if you are not doing it.

You need help Lyndsay before you no longer have any choices. You know the correct choice in a lot of instances, but you are not able to execute. You have such a strong need to be seen as someone who is able to do it all, to come up with a good idea, to be recognized, to be held in high regard. You need to receive immediate help on multiple issues. If I didn't know you and simply had someone send me a written account or summary of your behavior, I'd suggest immediate and aggressive therapy. Because you're my daughter I'm wanting to be more hopeful, optimistic, and am so wanting to believe you are able to change.

I don't think that now. You most certainly need help to save yourself from you while you still have another day.

We love you Lyndsay and want the best for you. We're your parents and we see what's happening to you and want you back. Please seek and accept some help and make it a priority. You've said you would before and didn't do it. You're simply not able to do it yourself. There are several options and we'd like to meet with you this week to discuss them and make a plan together to act on it right away. You may not have another "tomorrow" Lyndsay.

Love,

Your parents

After receiving this letter, I got a wonderful job offer with a Fortune 50 company in California, and I was not going to leave without Lia. She applied to several jobs, received an offer, and left the job she loved for a mediocre one to join me in my move. Many people told us not to go, but I wanted a new start in a new city. We were both excited to start a new life together in a new city. However, when you are carrying baggage, it tends to follow you wherever you go, regardless of the locale. I was certainly traveling with more than just literal baggage.

"Let go and let me. It is I who makes all things new. But you must be willing to surrender, child. I will help you."

I slept most of the way as we drove from Atlanta to California, opening my eyes just enough to see what state we were in and pop another Xanax. Although I was excited about my new position, I was suppressing the pain on the inside of my heart. Somewhere deep inside my heart, I knew that I was using Lia. I could not bear that pain I felt, although I could not identify the source of the pain. I chose to continue to drown myself in substances in attempts to separate myself from the feelings that came with knowing what I was doing was not right.

"You cannot outrun me, my child. I will walk with you forever, but you must learn that my path is the safest place you can be. I will use this to give you a new heart. I will use these trials to remove from you a heart of stone and give you a heart of flesh. For I know what I placed within your heart while you were in your mother's womb. You will see security is in me alone. I am constant. I will never leave you. Though you chose to run, I will pursue you. I will walk before you. I will protect you. You have a beautiful heart. You have my heart. It will be used to glorify me as you learn the safety and security of my undying love for you. Your loving heart will be used to share with others that security is in me and me alone; for I am your lighthouse in the darkness. I will use you to carry shine a bright light for those in darkness to lead them to me."

I spent my days working hard and accumulating knowledge in my new position with an amazing team. It was challenging, and I doubted my ability to perform at times, but I remained determined and enjoyed the variety of interesting tasks and the independence I was given. During this time, I was also starting the dissertation process for my Ph.D. Thus, I worked constantly, sometimes 16 hours a day.

I gave Lia little attention during the week, as I remained focused on my performance at work and school, but on the weekends, we loved exploring our new city. Drinking often was part of our routine, which did not always end well. Oftentimes, she played babysitter just as she had in Atlanta.

Despite my struggles, I read daily devotions here and there, kept a prayer journal, prayed with Lia on occasion, and we went to church, although infrequently. The Lord allowed me to place Fourth runner-up in a national pageant that year. My platform was human trafficking. *(Side note: You will see the coincidence of this in future publications given the Lord instructs me to continue sharing this part of my testimony!)*

"I want you to learn I am your platform, my daughter. When you learn this, I will be able to use you wherever I lead you. I will teach you that you are not only my princess, but my warrior and bride. Stand on my Word, my child. Stand on me. I hold you up; all else is fleeting."

I also had the opportunity to travel to ten countries that year and host a television show related to music. But despite my accomplishments, travels, and adventures site-seeing in a new state and multiple countries, I was still not in a great state of mind. On top of my past baggage which I had stuffed in the closet, I felt guilt from being in a relationship with a woman, fully aware that I was not a lesbian.

I adored Lia as a person. She had a beautiful heart and constantly forgave me as she knew I had struggles. She always told me she saw the good in me. However, I knew my motives were impure. I became aware that my decision to move with her to

California had not been the right choice. I was simply afraid to be alone in a new environment or not in a relationship. I was simply—broken. But I also felt it was too late to get out of the situation. Thus, I started acting out in various ways that were very hurtful not only to her, but to myself.

I have had to ask the Lord for forgiveness and forgive myself for leading Lia into a new city for my own selfish needs, as she was very happy in Atlanta near her family and friends with a job she loved. She began to get depressed, but I did not want to hear about how she felt. I did not want to communicate in general. It hurt too badly. My choice form of communication with her was drinking together, when it seemed much easier to have an excuse to pretend that everything was okay. However, I was simply stuffing the guilt I felt. It was the way I had learned to cope. And in the morning, when I was filled with that guilt I had yet to surrender to Jesus, she forgave me for my actions that occurred in the early morning hours after a late night of drinking, the hours when I was completely blacked-out—the hours I could not remember, nor did I want to. I did not want to hear the truth. I wanted to let it remain in the darkness; but it is in bringing the truth to the light that you experience true freedom.

Yes, the baggage of my bondage was seeping into her life, yet I still found security in my job, my education, and the fact that I brought in a nice income. I had dragged Lia along into my mess due to my own insecurity. The Lord did not want me in this relationship, He did not want Lia hurting or being used, and He wanted to protect me from additional bondage.

"Wait on me. I have a perfect plan as you travel along the path of righteousness with me as your lighthouse."

I was not on the right path during this time. I was straying—straying far from God's plan. At one point, I literally wandered off for three days, continuing to make reckless decisions. I was stumbling in the darkness. I broke my elbow one night and had to get another cast. I was, as someone once said, "a beautiful mess." What had been festering on the inside for so long was starting rearing its ugly head in apparent ways. I could not hide the pain anymore.

One day, Lia told me it was over; she had found a job in Atlanta. I was beyond hysterical. I went out with some friends that night and drank excessively while on more pain medication for my elbow. I went to a tattoo parlor that had already closed and begged them to tattoo "L^2" on my right ankle. After offering them $200, an outrageous price for a letter and a symbol, I got the tattoo, which was my attempt to somehow prove to Lia that I wanted to be with her. I was desperate—desperate for approval and love that I already had in Christ and had somehow forgotten!

"Again, I will remind you, Lyndsay. My love is endless and endures forever. I will shower you with my love. Again, I will rescue you."

After getting the tattoo, I wandered away from my friends and went into a random bar by myself. I told a lesbian couple that tonight was the night that I had decided I was going to kill myself. They followed me home to keep an eye on me, but when we arrived, Lia was not there. She was never *not home*. After the girls who had followed me home discarded the medication I planned on taking to end it all, I swallowed more than

133

just a handful of pills I had hiding in in the back of my medicine cabinet.

I do not remember much after this point. I called a close girlfriend in Atlanta, but I do not remember our conversation. Right after that, someone I did not know called my cell phone looking for a friend I had been with earlier that night. This friend of mine had used my phone earlier in the night after his phone died. I assume he must have called this person. Although I do not remember what I said to this stranger who called, I must have told him I had just taken the pills. Perhaps a part of me wanted to live.

He asked me where I lived and if he could come over to check on me, and I somewhat remember telling him my address. He hung up then called back soon after, stating he was nearby and had already arrived at my complex. At that point, I was more than just feeling the effects of the medication. I do not remember getting into the elevator to meet him downstairs to let him in, but I do remember what I saw when the elevator door opened.

As the elevator door opened, I fell into an EMTs arms. A group of EMTs then attempted to revive me, although I do not remember this. The last thing I remember was the horrible salts they placed near my nose to revive me along with the pain I felt in my chest where they had attempted CPR. My life had been saved.

I woke up the next morning in a hospital bed, half conscious, with a woman I did not know sitting by my bedside. I was on suicide watch. I vaguely remember her noticing I was somewhat awake and telling me my father was on the phone and she needed to verify it was him. As I dozed in and out of consciousness, I finally heard her repeated attempts to get my attention: "We need to verify this is your father on the phone, Lyndsay. What is the answer to a question that only he would know?" she asked. I somehow mumbled, "Ask him the email password he helped me set up in college. He will know the answer." I told her the answer, she asked him the question, and he responded correctly as I dozed back asleep.

When I woke up, my father had already flown from Atlanta to California and was sitting by my side in the hospital bed. Lia had also come to visit me. All I can remember is showing them my new tattoo, but they were just happy to see I was alive.

While unconscious, the Lord had spoken life over me as He saved it. I woke up repeating these words, "I changed the meaning of the tattoo I got last night. It now means "Lyndsay^2" because God gave me another chance at life and love!"

And that, He did! I am so grateful God had a beautiful plan for me although I could not see this at that time! I am so blessed He keeps His amazing promises!

Thank you, Lord, for your miraculous power! Thank you, Lord, for this testimony of hope, trust, faith in you, and your resurrection power!

Yes, God had saved me from myself and the plans of the enemy. Years later, I heard the Lord tell me I was "an emergency case" and He was the one that saved me. It was not within His will that I would try to take my life, but despite my attempts to take it myself, He graciously gave me another chance at life because of His love.

Today, well over ten years later, I am living life fully alive in Christ, and I am so thankful that He chose to save a sinner like me, despite all my poor choices many years ago. I know that it was His resurrection power that rescued me so that I could be used to rescue others.

Yes, I ran from God's will. I ran from God's plan. I ran from God's protection. I ran from His warnings and His pleas, including the pleas of those whom He was using to gain my attention, warn me, and love me, especially my dear family. But He saved my life. Like the father in the Parable of the Prodigal Child in the Word of God, my father and family accepted this prodigal child back into their home with open arms and love. The Lord always brings His prodigal children home.

As I traveled back to Atlanta, with my father by my side, I felt safe. I felt loved. I had left my family and flown to the other side of the U.S. and continued along my path of self-destruction, but my Heavenly Father had been with me every moment, and He never let me go.

Although earlier that week I was lying in a hospital bed for several days, my Heavenly Father saw His beautiful bride. He saw His warrior princess. His loving eyes saw all I was made to be; the things He had planned before I was in my mother's womb. He saw my true identity as His child. He saw my destiny; a destiny He had planned; one that was exceeding above my expectations. He did not see a victim; He saw a victor.

Despite all the things I could not yet see—despite my sin and filth—my Heavenly Father saw sweet victory.

He was not ready to take me to my eternal home. It was time to go back to home in Atlanta, with my father holding one hand, and my Heavenly Father holding my other. Yes, I was seated at the right hand of the King of Kings; but as far as here on Earth, there was much more work to be done For His Kingdom. He knew I was born to be an Overcomer, to share His gospel, and to be a vessel of His truth and a testimony of His miraculous power!

Yes. A living and breathing miracle! All that He did for me was paid for by His son, Jesus Christ, my First Responder who responded before I even asked for His help—the one who descended from the Heavens in a miraculous way to pay the debt for my sins before He ascended to His throne. Now, I boast in the cross, I boast in my weakness, and I give Him all the glory for sparing my life and for giving me "another chance at life and love."

I am a walking miracle and living proof of His resurrection power because of the power of the name of Jesus, and I will spend the rest of my life giving my all to Him because of what He gave to me before I was born. My mess of my past is now a message of God's grace, forgiveness, and love. My past trials have turned into to triumphing over the enemy's plans. And that test that put me in the emergency room? It is now just a part of my amazing testimony—simply because of the grace of God.

They triumphed over him by the blood of the Lamb and by the word of their testimony; they did not love their lives so much as to shrink from death.
~Revelation 12:11

I praise the Lord for allowing me to continue the book of my life that day. I praise the Lord for giving me an amazing testimony. I can assure you this is only a glimpse of the powerful testimony he gave me as an Overcomer in Christ, who truly is our Lighthouse, even in what seems the darkest of times! But in those dark moments, He draws us closer, guides us to safe harbors, holds us in His arms, and shows us that He is the brightest light of all. After all, lights shine brightest in the darkness.

What a beautiful thing, when even in our weakest moments… when we feel we are standing alone in the dark… the Lord is our Lighthouse, ushering us to safety and a place of joy and purpose, simply because of His unconditional, unlimited love. There is no distance to far for Him to go to rescue us. In rough waters, the lighthouse of His perfect love remains forever; He is the light that guides us and never grows dim. What a beautiful thing, when He erases the distance we feel from His love simply by washing us with grace, despite our struggles, trials, imperfections, and weaknesses. We can swim in the ocean of His forgiveness, grace, and love for eternity. As we do, the light within us as carriers of Jesus Christ become brighter and brighter. He is the God of many more than just "second chances at life and love." He is love, and in Him, He makes all things new. He is the sunlight blazing at midnight, the fire that quenches our thirst, the Alpha and the Omega for eternity, and the miracle maker who makes the impossible possible.

Epilogue

Dear Reader,

Having time off from school one summer and wanting to celebrate Lyndsay's progress in her recovery after an inpatient rehabilitation program, we both boarded a plane to Italy and took a cruise to Greece.

It became very clear to me at this time that her road to recovery still had many more miles to go. Desperately needing to spend time with the Lord, I took my Bible and journal and sat at the most forward section of the ship.

It was quiet there with only the blue water in view ahead of me. I poured out my heart to the Lord, looking for solace and to still my thoughts of worry and fear. He soon led me to look to my right where the height and beauty of the mountain laid. In my spirit, I heard Him say, "I can move mountains. I am a mountain-moving God." **I instantly knew this was His voice.**

Yes, I had mountains in my life, but more importantly, Lyndsay did. As much as God assured me she would become a mighty warrior as a young child, He assured me the mountains in her life **would** *be removed.*

As sad as I was through these turbulent years, God always told me He was our Healer, her Healer, though the process was not instantaneous.

I remember crying out to the Lord one night, saying, "I can't take this agony anymore! You have to come here now, Jesus!" At that very moment, the phone rang. I heard her voice and was assured that He was still holding on to her and at work in her life.

*To our readers, all I can say is this. Know **NOW** who Jesus is. Learn of Him and His Word **NOW**. For when a crisis comes, He **WILL** speak to your heart and fulfill those promises He made in a supernatural, miraculous way.*

Jesus truly is Lord….and a mountain moving God.

~Susan Wrensen, M.A.

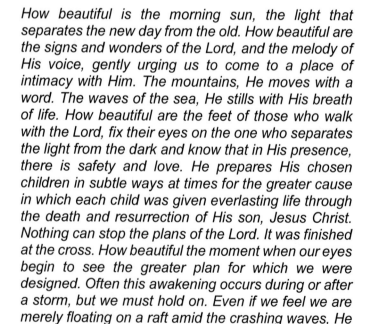

How beautiful is the morning sun, the light that separates the new day from the old. How beautiful are the signs and wonders of the Lord, and the melody of His voice, gently urging us to come to a place of intimacy with Him. The mountains, He moves with a word. The waves of the sea, He stills with His breath of life. How beautiful are the feet of those who walk with the Lord, fix their eyes on the one who separates the light from the dark and know that in His presence, there is safety and love. He prepares His chosen children in subtle ways at times for the greater cause in which each child was given everlasting life through the death and resurrection of His son, Jesus Christ. Nothing can stop the plans of the Lord. It was finished at the cross. How beautiful the moment when our eyes begin to see the greater plan for which we were designed. Often this awakening occurs during or after a storm, but we must hold on. Even if we feel we are merely floating on a raft amid the crashing waves, He calms the waters and whispers, "Be still, and know

that I am God." That life raft may be the precise device needed to bring us to the new land to which we were called.

Afterword

Each of us have decisions and choices to make on a daily basis, and how we respond shapes the journey we call life. Some decisions are more routine, trivial, and carry little consequence. Other decisions may have lasting impact and consequence that we may deal with the rest of our lives. Certainly, such decisions can be good or poor, but they nevertheless shape our lives for better or worse. I suspect many individuals are more inclined to think in the moment— short-term, with the desire to meet more immediate needs and gratification. Some are able to more carefully consider the ramifications of their decisions and determine that which better coincides with their longer-term goals and aspirations.

Sometimes, despite making a poor decision, we have the opportunity to pick ourselves back up and try a second time. This memoir of the writer's life is about having a second, perhaps even a third choice, to make improvement on the journey of life. It is not only a glimpse of what and where poor decisions can lead, but also to see what is possible when good decisions are made. Perhaps even more importantly, it is one person's story of how our Lord does not give up on us, even when we may have, and He intercedes and rescues us from a path of destruction, in order for us to become all of what He intended for our lives. This is about the intersection of our Lord's intervention and our exercise of free will and how He answers when we call His name.

This memoir of recollections portrays how Christ continues to pursue us, and in some cases saves us from acting only on our free will. I feel so blessed to have witnessed this transformation in my daughter, and I hope the reader will be encouraged, perhaps in a time of great fear and disillusionment, that all is possible.

~George Wrensen, M.A., C.A.S.

Acknowledgments

Thank you, Lord, for showing me where you were in every dark moment, for teaching me to trust, and giving me the boldness to share this portion of my story. You are my Life Saver and Savior.

To my father, for everything you have done for me. Thank you for your willingness to serve the Lord by not only being used to protect me, but to help guide me, and for coming to my rescue over and over again throughout my life. It means so much to me that you were strong enough to read each chapter I wrote over the past few years, even though some of it was hard to hear. Thank you for your love. I could not ask for a more perfect father for me. I love you so much.

To my mother, for your endless prayers, your faithfulness to God, and for teaching me His ways. Thank you for being there for me always. You have always been one of the strongest intercessors in my life. Words cannot express my gratitude to you. You have the heart of a servant. I love you beyond words, mom.

To my loving, beautiful sister, I am so happy that today you are in my life in a way that I know is how God wanted it all along! I am so thankful that today I am the big sis I was meant to be to you. Your love, encouragement, prayers, and support mean more than words can express. You are my best friend forever. I love you with all my heart. Thank you for never giving up on me and loving me for who I am.

To my sweet Auntie, for all your assistance in helping me with not only edits, but your countless prayers for our family over the years. I love you so much.

To Dan Johnson, thank you for allowing to Lord to use you as His mighty prophet. The words you spoke over me have come to pass. Thank you for your support, mentorship, and teaching in the prophetic.

To my bestie, Kris, thank you for being a powerful prayer warrior, loving sister in Christ, and for keeping in line. I ran from publishing this, but your words kept running through my mind. I'm so glad we get to spend eternity together.

To Dewayne Crowder, my friend I have "never met." You supported this book from day one. I am so thankful for all the times you have been there for me. Thank you for praying on my behalf. I treasure our friendship.

To Kris Cavanaugh, thank you for showing me the steps to make this happen and for being such an amazing example of a faithful servant. I love your heart for ministry. Your prophetic words mean so much to me. Without your assistance, I would never have published this.

To Peter Swanson, for speaking to me on the night I formatted this book that was accepted for publication almost three years ago. It was Christmas night. You are an amazing man of God. Thank you for your beautiful prayer.

To the prophetic team at Life Center Ministries, thank you for releasing the words you did years ago about the book of my life.

To the prophetic ministries' prayer team at International House of Prayer for allowing God to speak through you about God's purpose for my life years ago.

To Logos Global Network, thank you for your words in 2014 when I first went into ministry. The powerful word that a man who I don't even know shared with me was powerful and received.

Thank you to the countless number of others that God has used alone the way. Some of them are mentioned in this book, although their names have been changed, and others may not be mentioned here, but the Lord certainly knows how you helped.

About the Author

Please visit LivingLifeFullyAlive.com to read more about
the author.